"It's a genuine delight to see useful, practical tactics for living a happier life coming out of Hollywood screenwriting theory. *Change Your Story, Change Your Life* mines the screenwriter's language of motivations, intentions, and goals to show how you can radically reorganize the story of your life. Good screenwriting is good psychology, and it turns out you can actually get a handle on your life problems by approaching them as an ongoing story that you can rewrite and direct for a better effect."

— Christopher Vogler, Hollywood Development Executive; author: *The Writer's Journey*

"*Change Your Story, Change Your Life* is enlightening and moving, immensely practical in its application, and inspiring in its approach to overcoming the wounds and fears that keep us from what we truly want. But the book's greatest strength comes from Jen Grisanti's honesty and vulnerability. In bravely sharing the losses and setbacks that led to her ultimate success, she doesn't just lead you to your destiny; she takes the journey with you."

— Michael Hauge, Hollywood story expert and script consultant; author: *Writing Screenplays That Sell* and *Selling Your Story in 60 Seconds: The Guaranteed Way to Get Your Screenplay or Novel Read*

"In a sea of self-improvement books, Jen Grisanti's *Change Your Story, Change Your Life* uniquely turns the power of storytelling inward to help anyone — everyone — understand that the stories we tell ourselves *about* ourselves can either hold us back or make us truly free. Combining thoughtfulness, years of storytelling expertise, and a bottomless wellspring of humanity and love, Jen opens up about her own struggles and dares us to join with her to write and rewrite the story of us."

— Jeffrey Alan Schechter, screenwriter; author: *My Story Can Beat Up Your Story!*

"Who says you can't be the star of your own movie? In *Change Your Story, Change Your Life*, Jen Grisanti uses her expertise in story to help readers become the true 'main characters' of their own life script. And Jen should know. She lives her own story with such passion and focus that any one who reads her book should easily be inspired to do the same."

— Pilar Alessandra, screenwriting instructor: On the Page Screenwriting; author: *The Coffee Break Screenwriter*

"What an ingenious idea — to take the tools and techniques of story structure and apply them to our own lives to help us create and take charge of our own powerful stories! A deeply moving and inspiring read, by one of the brightest and most accomplished people in our industry."

— Steve Kaplan, creator of the HBO Workspace and the HBO New Writers Program; co-founder and Artistic Director of Manhattan Punch Line Theatre; author: *The Hidden Tools of Comedy*

"Reading this wise, insightful, and inspirational book not only helped my writing, it helped me deal with difficult life issues. If it's true that writing is the best therapy, then this is the therapist we all need."

— Pamela Wallace, screenwriter; producer; Academy Award-winning co-writer of *Witness*

"Jen's first book was one of the most important writing books I've ever read. *Change Your Story, Change Your Life* is one of the most important life books I've ever read. It's also, easily, the best sequel in Hollywood. Except for *The Bourne Ultimatum*. That was awesome."

— Chad Gervich, writer: *Dog With a Blog, After Lately, Cupcake Wars*; author: *Small Screen, Big Picture*

"Every writer knows that rewriting is infinitely easier than pounding out the first draft. Now in this brilliant book, Jen Grisanti shows us how we can apply the same principles to our own lives, taking a first pass that never quite comes together and turning it into everything we've ever wanted it to be."

— William Rabkin, Executive Producer: *Diagnosis Murder*; author: *Writing The Pilot*; Professor of Screenwriting, UC Riverside-Palm Desert

"Jen Grisanti's brave new book *Change Your Story, Change Your Life* is the most personal kind of loving gift a writer can offer. Straight from her heart to ours, it's a work of hope and guidance that reveals a very clear path toward a more meaningful life."

— Eric Edson, screenwriter; professor; author: *The Story Solution*

"Use your setbacks to create a more authentic life story. Grisanti's warm, honest voice, insight, and vulnerability make *Change Your Story, Change Your Life* exactly what you need to read when life pushes you to change."

— Kim Hudson, author: *The Virgin's Promise: Writing Stories of Creative, Spiritual and Sexual Awakening*

"In fiction, we often see the hero triumph in the end. Why? Because he or she follows the 'Rules of Story' and takes an active hand in his or her life. Hollywood story analyst Jen Grisanti gives you a road map to this process in *Change Your Story, Change Your Life.* Jen knows what she's talking about. She has lived it herself, in the movie biz and in real life. You don't have to be a screenwriter to use this terrific, spot-on book. It shows you how to be the hero of your own movie — and take it to a happy ending."

— Steven Pressfield, author: *The War of Art* and *Turning Pro*

"In stories, we know that most of the time the hero will ultimately achieve the goal. In our personal life story... that answer of whether we will achieve our goal is not always so apparent. In her new book *Change Your Story, Change Your Life,* veteran story executive Jen Grisanti shows us that despite possible setbacks and 'all is lost' moments, we have the ability within us to be the hero of our story — not the victim. Jen gives us tools on how we can achieve our goals despite these pitfalls and live the story and life we want to be living."

— Shawn Achor, author: *The Happiness Advantage*

"Jen Grisanti is the master alchemist of transformational narrative. In this book, which draws on the life experience of a storyteller, you will find a means to decode the power points and pressure points in the narrative of your life. It clearly and boldly grants you tools to transform your life story and claim your right to the title of hero. Treasure awaits the reader of Jen Grisanti's words."

— Stephen Lloyd Webber, author: *Writing from the Inside Out*; founder: Writing Immersion retreats

"*Change Your Story, Change Your Life* is a wise look at transforming the 'all is lost' moments of your life into the beginnings of achieving your true desire. Anyone who's experienced a loss will find comfort and strength in Jen Grisanti's powerful steps to creating a new life through creating a new life story. She combines classic storytelling principles with meaningful spiritual principles to guide you, step by step, toward achieving your fully realized life goals. From developing a clear intention, to changing the way you view conflict, to linking your story to success, you will get the tools you need to move from the darkest moments into the light and the life you deserve."

— Carole Kirschner, head of CBS Diversity Writers Mentoring Program; Director of WGA Showrunner Training Program; author: *Hollywood Game Plan: How to Land a Job in Film, TV or Digital Entertainment*

"In *Change Your Story, Change Your Life*, author Jen Grisanti uses her reversal of the adage 'art imitates life' to provide a creative, meaningful, and thought-provoking process on how each of us can combine life's toughest challenges with basic storytelling tools and exercises to gain the clarity and insight we need so we can make the changes for the happy, productive, and fulfilling life we each deserve."

— Kathie Fong Yoneda, story consultant; workshop leader; author: *The Script-Selling Game: An Insider's Look At Getting Your Script Sold and Produced*

"How many executives does it take to change a light bulb? Just one, when that one is Jen Grisanti. Let her show you how to light up your life."

— Ellen Sandler, writer/producer; author: *The TV Writer's Workbook*

"Those of us working in the entertainment industry are always looking for ways to tell better stories, more intriguing stories, and more meaningful stories. But Jen Grisanti, with her years of experience, has taken this one significant step further. How can we learn from the stories we tell? How can we use these tools to affect our own personal stories, our own lives? Can we actually stop, right where we are, look at our life story as it is unfolding, and make conscious decisions on how and why our story is evolving as it is? And, rather than letting our life stories determine who we are, can we determine who we wish to be by seeing our stories in a new and better informed light? Jen Grisanti has tapped into a powerful and empowering concept and you owe it to yourself to go on the journey with her. Change your story, change your life."

— Mark W. Travis, director, author: *Directing Feature Films, The Film Director's Bag of Tricks*

"Jen Grisanti has written a book in which storytelling, something writers engage in to relate outwardly, is turned back upon the creator. With *Change Your Story, Change Your Life*, she encourages and empowers readers to turn ego to spirit and meaningfully rewrite their own lives"

— Troy DeVolld, producer; author: *Reality TV: An Insider's Guide*

"Through the use of story, profound insights, and simple steps, Jen guides you to an awareness of your passions and strengths, so you can discover your niche in life. By aligning your personal and professional self, you can succeed and live with a more fulfilled sense of purpose from the inside out."

— Ann Baldwin, screenwriter; annbaldwin.net

"When you feel like you're losing momentum or direction on your life journey, pick up Grisanti's book. She's the big sister who sits you down and lovingly shows you how to get more from your next season of life. Her three-step process guides you to set clear intentions, redefine conflict, and experience success on your own terms. The exercises she offers are simple enough not to overwhelm; but complex in their gravity to generate the kind of deep introspection that transforms. Maybe you're at a place where you're asking yourself, 'What am I doing with my life? What do I do next? How do I even get there?' Start by reading *Change Your Story, Change Your Life*. With Grisanti's book, you will change your current story of fears, obstacles, dilemmas, and shattered pasts into a brand new story where you become the celebrated hero who captures her dreams!"

— Jennifer Dornbush, screenwriter; professor; author: *Forensic Speak*

"This book is a step by step guide to a life 'do over' — universally relatable and profoundly inspiring to anyone who has had the 'all is lost' moment."

— Jeanie Bradley, producer/TV executive

"Everyone is the main character of his or her own life story. But are you the hero, the villain, or the goat? What Jen Grisanti has brilliantly done in *Change Your Story, Change Your Life* is to take the principles of classic film narrative construction and teach the reader how to apply those principles to life as it is actually lived. For anyone struggling to figure out what their purpose is, to win that all-important victory, to live happily ever after, Grisanti will help you to give your own life the Hollywood ending you've always dreamed of!"

— Matt R. Lohr, co-author: *Dan O'Bannon's Guide to Screenplay Structure*; writer/creator: *The Movie Zombie* blog

Change Your Story, Change Your Life

A Path to Success

Jen Grisanti

Published by DIVINE ARTS
DivineArtsMedia.com

An imprint of Michael Wiese Productions
12400 Ventura Blvd. #1111
Studio City, CA 91604
(818) 379-8799, (818) 986-3408 (FAX)

Cover Design: Johnny Ink. www.johnnyink.com
Book Layout: William Morosi
Copyeditor: Matt Barber
Printed by McNaughton & Gunn, Inc., Saline, Michigan

Manufactured in the United States of America

Library of Congress Cataloging-in-Publication Data

Grisanti, Jen, 1966-
Change your story, change your life : a path to your success / Jen Grisanti.
pages cm
ISBN 978-1-61125-017-6
1. Motivation (Psychology) 2. Choice (Psychology) 3. Life change events. 4. Satisfaction. I. Title.
BF501.G75 2013
158--dc23

2013007144

Printed on Recycled Stock
Publisher plants 10 trees for every one tree used to produce this book.

Table Of Contents

To Mary Martin, my mom, for inspiring me by being an active hero in her battle against cancer, and for all of those who have endured or are enduring the same fight. May your triumph reflect the beginning of a new story; one that will be your gift to tell.

To my father, my brother, and my sister, for bonding together and uniting over our common goal to help mom get better.

Introduction

We all love a good story. Stories are a place where our imaginations can run wild and anything is possible, where we're inspired to believe in the idea of "happily ever after."

The stories we love the most begin when something dramatic happens that turns the main character's world upside down. Their life is thrown out of alignment, and they are forced to face and overcome dilemmas, obstacles, and "all is lost" moments, all ultimately leading to personal growth and the focused attainment of a chosen goal. We understand the negative consequences that will occur should they not achieve their goal, and we empathize with their journey, reacting emotionally when their goal is reached and they transcend to a higher level of self-understanding and personal fulfillment.

What if you could take the elements of "story" and apply them to your own journey? What if, after having been confronted with your own dramatic turning point, you could become the hero of your own story?

I'm here to tell you that you can. You've heard the saying that "art imitates life." In this book, I'm going to reverse that idea and show you how life can imitate art. I'm going to give you the tools and understanding needed to change your own story — and thereby change your life.

How do I know so much about story? I'm a veteran story consultant who has worked in building "story" for more than twenty years. I've read and consulted on thousands of scripts. I know what it is to construct a story worth telling, and how to elevate a story that isn't reaching its potential. I have the tools. But I also have the experience of successfully changing my own story.

My story in the entertainment business began in 1992 when I became an assistant to legendary television producer Aaron Spelling. For the next twelve years, Aaron was my mentor as I climbed the executive ladder at Spelling Television Inc., eventually running Current Programming, covering such shows as *Beverly Hills 90210*, *Melrose Place*, and *7th Heaven*. I was promoted to VP of Current Programming at CBS/Paramount in November of 2004, and while there I covered multiple shows, including *Medium*, *Numbers*, *Girlfriends*, and *NCIS*. It was my dream job, seemingly putting me one step away from the final goal that I had always envisioned: running a studio.

And then in May 2007, I faced my own turning point. I was told that my contract wasn't being renewed, and in that one moment my fifteen-year career was over. Virtually overnight, everything for me had changed. It was the end of one story and the beginning of another.

Pro • tag • o • nist [proh-tag-*uh*-nist] ***noun*** 1. The leading character, hero, or heroine of a drama or other literary work.

Life is a blank page. Each of us is the protagonist in our own story. Have you been confronted with a turning point that caused you to give up, to lose direction, to question everything? You can learn how to take a turning point and use it as a powerful place to begin your new story. You can identify new destinations and goals. You can face and overcome obstacles. You can survive your "all is lost" moments, and grow from them, moving from ego to spirit, to arrive at destinations better than anything you ever imagined. You can become the hero of your own story.

After my turning point, I turned negative into positive using the very story tools I taught. How I did that is what inspired this book.

Change Your Story, Change Your Life is about learning to create the life you desire by empowering the possibility of change after a major turn of events. For some, the shock of a sudden turn can paralyze all possibility. For others — as in the stories with heroes and heroines we love — the turn is an opportunity to move in a new, more meaningful direction, even if it doesn't appear as such at first. By learning how to apply story tools to my own life, I was able to learn how to change both my story and my life. I'm going to show you how to do the same. How to become the author of your own story. How to be the hero of your own life. How to write a new happy ending filled with deep internal meaning and fulfillment. I'm grateful that you've chosen to take this journey with me.

Let's begin!

CHAPTER ONE

TURNING POINTS

We must let go of the life we have planned,
so as to accept the one that is waiting for us.
— *JOSEPH CAMPBELL*

ARE WE EVER PREPARED FOR THE MOMENT WHEN OUR LIFE takes a turn and everything we know changes? I will never forget the day when my fifteen-year career as a studio executive came to an end. I was called into my boss's office. It was on the heels of a situation at work where I had made a choice to stand up to a difficult person. In the moment of this conflict, I acted on impulse. I had taken so many risks during my career to get where I was. At the time, I was so close to reaching my career destination. I'd had conversations like this one many times before, and my calculated risks had always paid off. I was promoted each time. This time was different. I could feel it. My life was about to change. I went into my boss's office and sat down. I felt like a child again, being called into the Principal's office. We started the uneasy small talk that was obviously leading to something big. And then it arrived. "Your contract comes up in December. We are not going to renew it." Even though I knew what was coming, it still was devastating to hear. In that moment my world turned upside down. I was no longer traveling in a specific direction. My dream — to run a studio — was hitting a dead end. (In "story" terms, this turning point was my "all is lost" moment. More on that later.)

One of the first things that I thought about in the midst of the shock and devastation was, "What did I do to contribute to this outcome?" In hindsight, I can see that somewhere along the way I had lost the momentum in my pursuit. I was a Vice President. I had hit a pinnacle. I only had a few more steps to go to attain my ultimate dream, but I was beginning to question what I wanted. The loss of momentum caused me to doubt the path I was on. In the race to the top, I was losing a part of myself. Being a high-level studio executive didn't seem to fit the picture I had imagined. While I loved the work of developing story on five shows every week and helping discover talented new writers, there were other things involved that didn't fall in alignment with who I was. In the moment that I made a choice and took an action that led to the end of my career, I thought that I was responding from my spirit. As I went through the growth process, I recognized that I had responded from my ego. I couldn't really respond from my spirit because, in that moment, my spirit was depleted. I had developed the wrong part of myself during my climb up the corporate ladder. I had been fueled by my ego, and had spent my spirit in the process. Now it was time to get it back.

I am sharing this particular life moment with you because this was the starting point of my new story. This was the turning point that led me to change my story and, in the process, to change my life. I made this change by utilizing the story tools that I had used with professional writers for my entire career. I'm going to share these tools with you, along with my own experiences and the experiences of others who hit a turning point and successfully turned the end of one story into the beginning of a new story. I want you to begin to think about which turning point is going to start your new story.

Right after my turning point, one of the first things I had to do was to redefine both my path and my identity. There were so many emotions to process. My destination was changing. I had gone through a divorce nine years earlier and, as a result, I had essentially re-married my job. So the end of my job felt like going through a second divorce. Oddly enough, I had fantasized about being in a situation where my job ended and I had several months left on my contract that would get paid out. I would actually get paid while not working. Did I manifest that situation? For seventeen years, since graduating from USC, I had worked on building my career. This was going to be the first time in my life that I could wake up in the morning and not have to be anywhere. I had so much time to fill. I knew that I had to take the time to heal before planning my new direction.

I asked myself this question: When life takes a sudden turn, can we change? Most of us spend the first part of our adult lives building a career. We make a plan and head in one very clear direction. We do the work. We hit the obstacles. We move through them. We see the light at the end of the tunnel. We evaluate what to do to get through the final stretch and attain our goal. After hitting so many obstacles, the possibility is within our grasp. But then something happens and, in an instant, our destiny is altered. Things turn upside down. It feels as if our story has ended. Yet, it could be the start of a new story. Can we rebuild? Yes, we can.

In the years that followed, I turned my "all is lost" moment into a gift that would open doors to opportunities I never imagined. I am now an international speaker, a story/career consultant, a blogger for The Huffington Post, and the author of three books. I have guided numerous writers on their path to success. Professionally, I am living my dream. My professional life is everything I'd hoped it would be and more. I was able to rebuild and recreate a new destination. It would not have happened unless I had hit rock bottom first. I didn't realize in the moment my world turned upside down that it was an experience that would formulate my voice and connect me with my audience.

Looking back, there were three key foundational steps that helped me to get from where I was back then to where I am today. I want you to consider these steps as you are writing and defining where your new story is going to begin. These will help you to move through your turning points, so put them to good use:

- Clear Intention
- Change The Way You View Conflict
- Link Your Story To Your Success

Clear Intention

After experiencing a life turn, you are often faced with a dilemma. You need to make a choice about your new direction. You may have lost a job, faced illness or disability, ended a marriage or relationship, or lost a family member. Your world is turned upside down. Setting a strong intention as to *why* you want to go where you want to go will determine your success in getting there.

In fiction, when you express why the central character is pursuing what they are pursuing, you give the audience a stronger sense of the internal side of their story. This is a valuable tool storytellers use to add more depth to the pursuit. By doing this, you also create internal stakes. You establish the potential negative consequences that could happen to the character if the goal isn't achieved. You can use this same insight to motivate you toward the goal in your own story.

What do you hope to gain internally from your external pursuit? Part of why you don't get the results you want — or soon discover that the end result is not what you thought it could be — is because you haven't clearly thought out *why* you want what you want before you go after it. You need to develop a strategy that links what you want internally with your external pursuit. This is a key point that I will repeat several times in several ways throughout the book because this is a very important tool in understanding how to write your new story and how to reach your external goal. Remember: if your emotional reasons for wanting to succeed aren't clear, you may find yourself lost after crossing the finish line.

On my own path, I found that by working on my intention and visualizing the desired outcome in any given situation, I was able to manifest the results I wanted. I learned to do the work that needed to be done to bring about positive results. How did I get such positive results? I learned how to utilize the very "story tools" I taught as a script consultant in a way that would help me to write the story that I wanted my own life to tell. By doing this, my world opened up. My potential suddenly didn't have limits. There was no glass ceiling. As my friend Star Ladin would say, I was experiencing success "on my terms."

Change the Way You View Conflict

At the point when I lost my job, I had read and consulted on thousands of scripts. I had seen protagonist after protagonist (i.e., the "hero" of a story) face conflict and move through what I refer to as the "all is lost" moment. This is the moment where the hero hits rock bottom and is as far away as possible from achieving their goal. In this moment of hitting rock bottom, the hero realizes what they need to do to attain the goal. I was hitting my "all is lost" moment in my own story. Upon hearing the words "we are not going to renew your contract," I was, in fact, as far away as possible from achieving my original goal.

During my journey of figuring out my new goal, I suddenly began to wake up to my true possibility. I could rebuild. I could define a new direction that was in better alignment with who I was internally. With this discovery, I began to see my obstacles, conflict, and turning points in a new light. In the moment, I viewed them as the worst thing that could happen. In hindsight, I see that they were actually the best things that could have happened. I needed a nudge, a gentle reminder that the direction I was traveling was no longer working for me. I could turn an end into a start. What an empowering idea this was for me! By changing my view toward conflict — by seeing conflict as a valuable directional indicator, rather than as a problem — I was beginning to change my story.

Link Your Story To Your Success

By learning how to write your story and be the author of your life, you will learn how to tell and sell your story. Understanding how to tell and sell your story, in turn, will create opportunities on so many levels. Believe me when I tell you this: Your personal story has everything to do with your professional success.

I've done work with groups of female entrepreneurs. At one specific event, I had the group write short, separate "summary lines" for their personal story and their professional story. Then I had them link the two together. The outcome was phenomenal. One woman got up on stage and was near tears. She said she realized that before this exercise, when asked what her business was and upon sharing it, she would get blank looks. People would not understand. She did not know how to tell her story. Through this exercise, she realized that she was not really telling people what her business was, because she wasn't linking her personal backstory that her audience needed in order to connect. By utilizing the story tools that I taught her, she suddenly had clarity in telling her own story. Having this type of epiphany after learning how to tell your story is what will lead you to your success.

When you share your story, you help people get to know you. I learned the true value of this during some of my first speaking engagements. When I began my talks, I'd introduce myself. I'd share my background as a VP at a top studio, and I'd mention that Aaron Spelling was my mentor, etc. What I came to recognize is that the majority of people can't connect with this story. Sure it adds to the credibility of what I am teaching, but it doesn't help people understand who I am. Only when I began sharing two turning points in my own life — a long relationship that ended in a short marriage, and the career-ending loss of a job — did I begin to see a transformation in the audience. People could connect with these life experiences. Knowing that I went through what so many of them have gone through connected us on a universal level and contributed immensely to the outcome of the event. This was a tool that made a world of difference. Using this tool in my public speaking sparked the "aha!" moment that our personal story is linked to our professional success.

By using your personal story in business and in life, you allow others to identify with you.

Story Tools

The following are some of the story tools and terms that you will need in becoming the author of your life. These tools will make you view your life turns in a new way. They will help you to become aware that with each life turn you experience, you have an opportunity to write a new story with a new goal that could bring you greater fulfillment than you ever imagined. By understanding how to apply these tools to your story, you will be able to write your story in a way that will inspire you to reach your external goal and change your story into one that reflects more of the life that you desire.

Protagonist/Hero — You are the protagonist; you are the active hero of your own story.

External Goal — As the protagonist of your own story, you will define an external goal. This is the physical form of *what* you want.

Internal Goal — As the protagonist, you will also think of an internal goal. This is *why* you want what you want.

Starting Dilemma — The moment that leads you to defining your external goal is referred to as a dilemma. Dilemmas are moments in your life when you are forced to make a decision between two choices, with neither choice being clearly "right." In story, all drama and comedy stems from a starting dilemma.

Thematic Question — Your dilemma and external goal are followed by the thematic question. Think of it as a debate that the writer is having with himself via the actions of his main character. The thematic question is part of the internal journey of why you want what you want.

"All Is Lost" Moment — This is the moment when you hit rock bottom while on the road to reaching your external goal. It is when you are as far away as possible from achieving your goal. It is often in this moment that you reach your "aha!" moment and recognize what you need to do to fully achieve your goal in the most meaningful way possible.

In my professional story, the starting dilemma I faced as a result of my "all is lost" moment was: Do I continue to climb the corporate ladder knowing that I am putting my destiny in someone else's hands, or do I go out on my own and start my own business? I made the choice to start my own business. Building my business into something big was my external goal. It stemmed from my "all is lost" moment, which turned into my starting dilemma in my new story. "All is lost" moments can lead you toward your goal once you learn how to become the hero in your own story. They are the moments that create change.

The thematic question I pondered in this process was, "Can I change my story and, in the process, change my life?" As a studio executive, my job was to help writers elevate their stories by giving them story notes. As I began to see myself as the hero in my own story, I could hear the executive within giving myself the same notes. I'd say things like, "This is when you have the 'aha!' moment and realize what you need to do in order to attain the goal." In my story, I knew that my goal had to change. My initial plan and the direction my life was headed in had to change. I had to break down my old ways of thinking and construct a new path. I was no longer able to reach the destination I had planned on reaching. So, essentially, I had to take my "all is lost" moment and turn it into the starting dilemma of my new story.

I want you to think about the moments that I've mentioned in my story and use them as examples of moments that you can draw from in your story. Millions of you share my story. You've lost your job. You've divorced your spouse. Your children have left home. Illness or economic hardship has altered your way of living. You've hit a wall. You've lost your sense of balance. I know you. I understand your pain. I share in your journey. If you think about it, most of these situations that I mentioned are the starting points in great movies and television shows. Through the loss, you are forced to make a new plan, either in your personal or professional life. In order to design a new plan, you have to reevaluate what you want and why you want it. You have to do the work to heal and process the change. This way, you make choices from a stronger place of wisdom. You have to move from feeling threatened and fearful to finding truth and peace. This is your unique journey, but at the same time, your journey is universal. Remember: You are not alone.

Earlier I mentioned "summary lines." A summary line is a valuable story tool that I want to share with you. It's one of the first steps you'll take in writing your new story. For your story, let's call it your "life summary line." The components of your summary line are the following:

- Set-up of "who"
  (present the protagonist and their strengths/weaknesses)
- Dilemma
- Action
- Goal

Your life summary line is a brief synopsis of your "story arc" — the full arc of your entire life story, from its beginning to the present. Story arcs allow you to go into more detail. Throughout the book, I will refer to story arcs and summary lines as the life moments you experience that are milestones in your own story. By understanding how to chart certain life moments into arcs, you will be able to link what moments will connect to your success in any given situation. They could be the arc of what led you on your career path, the arc of what led you to get married, the arc of what led you to heal from a traumatic situation, the arc of a desire that you want to attain, the arc of a dream unrealized, and the list goes on.

After thinking about how to write your life summary line, I want you to familiarize yourself with how you are going from writing your life summary line to expanding it into your story arc. Your story arc is the road map tracing *how* you are going to travel from your starting turning point to the end of your story and the achievement of your goal.

Below are the elements that make up your story arc:

1. Starting dilemma
2. External goal stemming from dilemma
3. Thematic question
4. Actions taken
5. Obstacles hit leading up to your "all is lost" moment
6. External and/or internal stakes
7. Attainment of your goal

During the arc of any story, you see a protagonist's growth and transformation. A good story starts with a *dilemma* that forces the hero (you!) to make a choice. The choice is your *external goal*; it defines what you want. Then you may explore the *thematic question*, which stems from your dilemma. Upon making a choice, you devise a plan. By doing this, you are taking *action*. You will hit escalating *obstacles*, and oftentimes you will hit an *"all is lost" moment* when you are as far away as possible from achieving your goal. You will think about the *external stakes* in your story. What is the worst that can happen if you don't achieve your goal? By reminding yourself of these stakes in your arc, you will motivate yourself toward your goal. Lastly, in your arc, you will *attain your goal.*

Your life has many story arcs in it. Certain arcs stand out more because they often involve times of extreme joy or extreme loss and they contribute to the growth and success of your overall story. Let's look at a story arc in the movie *Hope Springs*, written by Vanessa Taylor. The story begins with the dilemma that Kay (Meryl Streep) faces after being rejected by her husband Arnold (Tommy Lee Jones) when she suggests that they sleep in the same bed again after years of sleeping in separate rooms. After celebrating their 31st wedding anniversary, Kay decides that she wants her marriage back. This is externally shown through the symbolism of a bed. This is the external goal that stems from the starting dilemma. The thematic question that Kay explores is "Can you change your marriage?" The inciting incident, the moment that triggers the change, is when she tells Arnold that she wants to go to Maine for a week and take intensive couples counseling with Dr. Bernie Feld (Steve Carell). The internal goal is to change their marriage, which is symbolized through them sharing a bed again. The obstacles hit are Arnold's resistance to the change and Kay's pursuit of the change. It is revealed that their trouble with intimacy started after their youngest child left for college. Arnold began to close his eyes during sex. The "all is lost" moment is when Kay and Arnold get over a number of obstacles and feel as if they're well on their way back to intimacy, but then Arnold opens his eyes during sex and looks at Kay and everything stops. He can't finish. They end the week with Dr. Feld without fulfilling the goal. As a result, Kay makes plans to leave the marriage. In reaction to this, Arnold steps up and goes into Kay's bedroom. Finally on the same wavelength, they are now able to kiss and have sex and renew the intimacy in their marriage, which leads to them renewing their vows and sleeping in the same bed again.

By turning your "all is lost" moment into your starting dilemma, you have a place from which to begin your story. You can turn an ending into a beginning. You can get your spirit back. You can change your story. "All is lost" moments are important to you because they are the starting points for your life summary lines and story arcs which will lead you to writing your new story.

Exercise One

What is the turning point from which you want to begin your new story? Choose one turning point you've recently faced that created a powerful dilemma. We will continue using this example as we proceed through the book.

CHAPTER TWO

MOTIVATION

Only as high as I reach can I grow, only as far as I seek can I go, only as deep as I look can I see, only as much as I dream can I be.

— KAREN RAVN

AFTER LOSING MY JOB, EXAMINING AND RE-DEFINING MY MOTIVATION was the key that opened up the next chapter in my life. In the moment of the loss, I felt as if my world was crumbling. I was hitting an "all is lost" moment. I had used discipline and commitment all of my life to get to this stage in my career. In an instant, it was gone. What was left was the value that I had created along my path. By tapping into this recognition, I had to motivate myself to design a new plan for what was next. I had been through a few "all is lost" moments before this in my personal life. At the beginning of my career, my parents announced that they were getting a divorce after 27 years of marriage. In this moment, my world felt shattered. In the heat of the loss, I started to question everything about my foundation. What did this all mean? Where did the love go? How were our lives going to move forward while not operating as one unit? How do we fill a hole that used to have 27 years of family in it? I knew we were still a family. We just had to find the motivation needed to establish a new way to be a family separately. I know that I am speaking for the masses in these life experiences. When the rug gets pulled out from under you, in either your personal or professional life, you may temporarily lose your motivation to move forward. You become frozen in the loss. You are humbled. You are vulnerable. It is in these moments that you really become aware of the ego versus the spirit. You learn that it is better to be motivated by your spirit. You gain tools from each experience. Motivation will be the tool that will help you to move forward.

"Motivation" derives from the word "motive" — "something (a need or desire) that causes a person to act." In fiction, "motivation" is a key ingredient in successful character development. What causes you to take action? What desire drives you in any given direction? When you act, you get results. Whether the results are good or bad, they help you to grow. It helps when you think about what the cost will be if you *don't* act, and what the reward will be if you *do*. If you focus on the actions of your past and the positive effects that were produced as a result, you can motivate yourself to act in the present.

In most fictional stories, there are five important elements of a central character's motivation. Think about these five components of motivation when looking at your own story:

- Desire
- Wound and Flaw
- External Stakes
- The Past
- Moving Forward and Evolving

Desire

In any story, the desire of the central character usually stems from what he or she dreams about. Through their words and actions, you often get a glimpse of what they want. This is before they hit any obstacles or before their world is turned upside down. Learn to utilize your desire.

It will fuel you and point you in the direction you want to go. It is a unique energy that helps you to clarify what it is that you want. Your desire will lead you down the right and the wrong roads. There will be something to learn no matter where it takes you. You just need to trust that it will help you to discover what it is you really want.

Think about what you want. What are the emotions behind what you want and why you want it? In conceptualizing your new story, go back to a time when you were innocent, before knowing that everything you set out to do wouldn't always work in your favor. What did your desire look like before it got knocked down, rejected, and lost its way? How did it make you feel to visualize what you desired, leading you exactly where you wanted to go without hitting any roadblocks? Move into this feeling. Draw from it. Recreate it. Think about it now.

How do you view that desire differently now that you've gained wisdom from past experiences in which obstacles seemed too big to overcome? What did it feel like to stop moving toward your goal? What was the obstacle that was the final straw? What if you could learn to trust that your desire will lead you where you need to be? At this point in life, you know that you're going to hit walls, that often these obstacles will escalate, and that you may hit what is referred to as an "all is lost" moment. As in any story, whether it be real or scripted, you know that when you hit rock bottom and are as far away from reaching your goal as possible, you can still pick yourself up and accomplish the goal. Your desire will still be by your side at the end. Your desire is what will pull you through. You just need to learn to trust that it is steering you in the right direction. Obstacles are part of the journey on the way to a dream. The dream wouldn't be a dream if it were easy to attain. Befriend your desire and know that it will steer you where you are meant to go. All you have to do is follow it.

WOUND AND FLAW

The second thing I want you to look at in terms of your story and your motivation is the idea of "wound and flaw." Often your wounds come from the moment your world is turned upside down and your desire suddenly feels as if it's drowning. You want to reach for it, you want to pull it to safety, but you have lessons that you need to learn before it can be completely safe again. You have to move into understanding what those lessons are. When you live in your wounds, flaws appear. Your flaws can get in the way of taking your desire the full distance. Your flaws are often emotional reactions or emotional blocks that come from your wounds. When you feel like something was taken from you, you get angry. Anger is a flaw. When you feel your momentum hit a wall, you see being active as painful, so you become passive. You decide that it is easier to react than to act. Passivity is a flaw. You can learn to use your wounds and your flaws to push you forward versus hold you back. When you feel defeated, you do things to sabotage your success. All of this is part of your path and put there so you learn what you need to know to get over the obstacle and add more "perseverance" tools to your toolbox. As life goes on, your obstacles will become greater. If you learn how to use your pain to drive you forward, you will be ahead of the game. It's about believing that there will be a light at the end of your tunnel of darkness and your desire will continue to ignite your possibility and pave the way to your dream.

When I work with writers on their stories, I ask them to think about the wound that drives each character and the flaw that gets in the way. I learned about the idea of the wound from the screenwriting author Michael Hauge. It helped me to hit an "aha!" moment in the way that I see story construction. What are your wounds and your flaws? When you are able to identify them, you are able to see the internal obstacles you create that get in the way of your drive. Sometimes your own fears are your flaws and they sabotage you from getting what you want. These fears often come from your wounds. This reminds me of a great quote I saw posted on Facebook: "We don't need to be wise beyond our years. All we need to do is be wise beyond our fears." It's about learning to move toward your fears instead of away from them. Your wounds can be used to drive you forward instead of leave you in limbo. It's all up to how you react. What wounds could drive you forward instead of hold you back?

External Stakes

The third component of motivation, one that writers often miss or don't build out in their fictionalized story, is the external stakes arc. In story, when an external stakes arc is well developed you know all during the story what is the worst thing that can happen if the goal is not achieved. You can visualize and feel the metaphorical death that can transpire if you do not protect your desire and move it toward its destination. When this is done well in film and TV, you keep an eye on the goal and no matter how big the hurdles get, you know that your protagonist will find a way to finish the race.

What if you applied this to your own life? What if you really thought about what the external stakes arc is in your own story? What if you remind yourself of the metaphorical death that you will experience if you don't finish the race? You can visualize that by knowing what your stakes are, you can stay on the path and move over the hurdles on your way to the finish line. How gratifying would your finish be if you didn't hit the hurdles and if you didn't have the gentle reminders of why it is so important for you to create your dream? Do you want your life to end with a bunch of dreams that were never realized? If you don't, then it will help you to always keep your external stakes present in your story.

For me, the external stakes after losing my job included not being able to work with writers again, losing my dream of working in the entertainment business, losing my value in the market, not being able to afford my current lifestyle, and fearing that I would have to rely on my parents for financial help if I didn't figure out a new path. My external stakes made me imagine the worst outcome possible if I didn't find the motivation and figure out how to pick up the pieces. By doing this, I was able to draw from my spirit and gain the strength and confidence to believe that I could do it. I could redefine my path and build a future, only this time it would be on my own terms.

The Past

You are often driven by something that was lacking in your past. You were hurt. You were lost. You felt isolated. You were made to feel "less than." You were told that it would never happen. Then later, people came into your path and encouraged you to believe in yourself. They helped you to shut out the noise and see your potential. They saw your gift before you did. They nurtured your possibility. You learn how to use all of these emotions to catapult you forward. You begin to recognize that you want to experience pleasure and move out of pain. Pain can be a motivator. You learn to use pain to see what doesn't work and help you to better define what does. You are motivated. When you learn to identify with what drives you, you can become more active in your life. Your level of activeness comes down to the choices you make. You can create the destiny of your choosing. You just have to be clear on what this is and be an active participant in your story.

Going back to when you started formulating some of your life goals, what do you recall went into these decisions? Why was it important for you to accomplish what you wanted to accomplish? Did you want to feel a sense of achievement? Did you want to provide security in your life? What did security look like in your childhood? Did you feel it enough of the time? Was security connected to money? Or was it connected to emotional balance and doing what you loved? What rewards did you seek in deciding the direction in which you wanted your life to go? What wounds were driving you? What flaws did you allow to get in the way? Who was a part of making you believe that anything is possible? What emotions did you attach to the desired outcome? Did you move in the right direction? Did you accomplish some of those life goals you dreamed of? Or did you let logic and practicality outweigh the dream? Are you living your dream now? If not, could you be? By writing your story, you can reach your dream. It all comes down to strategizing a plan that will get you to your end destination.

You start formulating your goals during childhood at a time when belief that anything is possible is a large part of your existence. You watch your parents work hard, and you see the fruits of their efforts in the way they live. They either pay off or they don't. You see first-hand the pleasure and the pain behind their dream. You may decide to go on a similar path based on what you see. Or you decide to go in the complete opposite direction because you witness first-hand how the work far outweighs the dream that your parents were striving to achieve. You may have grown up rich, middle class, or poor. You absorb all of this and, as a result, you decide what your own future path will look like. You connect with the root of what caused your pain and what you believe will bring you joy. You use the past to motivate you into the present and on to the future. You think about the quality of life you had as a child and the quality of life you desire as an adult. Did the path taken by your parents motivate you to go down the same path, or move you in a different direction?

Through my own experience, I've learned that you can see the past from another perspective and, in essence, change the way you see it. When you think about your childhood memories, you remember your side of the experience. You create mental blocks based on your recollection of the moment. Try asking the people who were there about how they recall the same moment; you might find that they have a different perspective of it. This could change the way you view it.

I'll give you an example. I recall having a memory of a huge pivotal moment in my childhood. When I became an adult, I thought I began to see it more clearly. I attached a feeling to the memory that was holding me back a bit. Then I had a conversation with my mom. I told her about it. She told me her recollection. One thing that she said changed everything. I was viewing it in the wrong way. I was seeing the memory from a child's perspective and only viewing my side of it. When she opened it up, I began to see it from a totally different perspective. This freed me. This allowed me to change the story that I was holding on to for so long. The memory of the wound began to heal. My personal narrative shifted. As I said earlier, flaws often stem from your wounds. When your flaws come into play, they often can sabotage you, getting in your way and preventing you from attaining what you want. The negative talk in your mind tends to dominate. Your flaws are what make you human. So, in understanding your own flaws and how you can use them to your advantage instead of a deterrent to your dreams, you can learn how to draw from your old wounds, learn from your flaws, and move in the direction that you want your life to go.

Moving Forward and Evolving

In creating a new life goal, let's talk about moving from ego to the spirit. When you start in the ego, you want to achieve the dream for selfish reasons. Then you hit obstacles, some of which open you up to the idea that maybe your philosophy and how you see things in a certain particular situation isn't really serving you. You begin to evolve and, as a result, you move into the spirit. When you are operating from the spirit, you move into the divine. You experience a higher consciousness that views the achievement of the goal without limits. The achievement isn't just about you anymore. It expands beyond how it can help you into how it can help the greater good and benefit others. Instead of just tying your possibility to a title, a salary, a bonus, or a pension, you begin to see that your worth is about so much more. You feel a message coming through you and know that it is up to you to deliver it. If you can achieve in a way that sends out a message and becomes not just about you and the attainment of your goal, but about the greater good and the betterment of others, then you'll begin to move in a more authentic direction. You'll "follow your bliss" and the rewards may come in different ways, but the rewards often feel more fulfilling when you are able to make this transition.

I like to give writers this story tip: For the first three-quarters of their story they should have the central character respond from the ego, and for the last quarter they should have them respond from the spirit. With this thought process, the central character transforms from where he/she was at the beginning of the story to the person they become at the end. I cannot tell you how many writers love this tool because it helps them show how their character grows through the journey of the story. Understanding how to use this tool will allow you to see your growth in your own story.

The HBO series *Enlightened* embodies this idea of shifting from the ego to the spirit. The series revolves around Amy Jellicoe (Laura Dern), a woman who goes through a spiritual transformation after an affair with her boss blows up in her face and results in her being demoted to a lower division at the company she works for. After the trauma, Amy takes a trip that transforms her in a spiritual way. She brings the lessons of this trip home with her. In one of my favorite episodes titled "The Weekend," written and directed by Mike White, Amy desperately wants her ex-husband Levi (Luke Wilson) to be a part of her spiritual awakening. She wants him to want to change like she is doing, and specifically to stop using drugs. Amy suggests that they go on a kayaking trip for the weekend and, despite being against it, Levi agrees. There are two sequences of voice-over by Amy that perfectly depict the concept of moving from ego to spirit. The first happens as they are kayaking down the river. As Amy watches Eli, she ponders, "My first love, my husband, my heartbreak, my pain. It feels so easy now, here. You're not the cheat and the liar. I'm not the nag and the shrew. We're not old or young. There's no bitterness or illusions. No need for fear or hope. We're just spirits drifting through this perfect rift together. We can be free of our sad stories. They float away until they are like memories of a dream from the night before, shadows under the water of what's left in our life. Life is a gift...." At this point, Amy wants

Levi to move with her in this spiritual awakening. Then she discovers that Eli has brought drugs with him on the trip. Amy is faced with the reality that Eli hasn't changed. Her next voice-over dialogue reflects this new awareness: "You can try to escape the story of your life, but you can't. It happened. The baby died. The dog died. The heart broke. I knew you when you were young. I know your heart broke too. I will know you when we are both old and maybe wise. I hope wise. I know you now, your story. Mine isn't the one that I would have chosen in the beginning, but I'll take it. It is my story. It's only mine and it's not over. There's time. There is time. There is so much time...."

This episode resonated with me on so many levels. The depth of emotion and spirit of the words written by Mike White blew me away. The words and the visuals had a magical effect. They spoke to me. They made me remember my past story. They made me forgive. They made me feel. They brought me back to the innocence of the beginning where everything starts. Like millions of others, I know what it's like to experience betrayal in a marriage and to feel broken. I know what it is to go through unexpectedly losing a job, although not in the same context as Amy. I realized in watching this episode that the masses go through these experiences and witness the same emotions that come from them. Our stories are different, but our emotions are the same. I believe that when we detach from our ego and connect with our spirit, we find our voice. Our voice is what connects us to others. Our voice leads us to becoming enlightened.

Personal and Professional

When you assess your life, you typically look at two major areas: the personal and the professional. You may find that you are very happy in one area of life, but not the other. Very often the professional domain takes precedence in your life over the personal, or vice versa. As a result, one area of your life may not be as prosperous as it could be. So, when you go into setting new goals to start your story, you need to look at these two sides and figure out a balance. How can you learn to get what you want professionally while getting your emotional needs met personally? I would say that this is a universal life quest.

If you're like me, the professional accomplishments feel so comfortable and attainable. My professional life feels safe, while my personal life feels so far away, like a distant dream. I remember during one seminar I did for my book *Story Line: Finding Gold In Your Life Story*, a woman asked me, "Do you feel betrayed by the business world?" It was in response to a question I had asked the class earlier, which was "Have you ever been betrayed?" I answered her and said, "Yes, I do feel betrayed by the business world." I thought back to the day — after fifteen years of working with the same company, having a very successful track record and strong relationships — of hearing the words "Your contract ends in November. We are not going to pick it up." This was in May of that year. I felt my dream dissolve in that moment and everything that I had built up to that point was beginning to vanish. I got very defensive. My security was being taken away from me, and I felt very concerned. This was on the heels of a situation at work that led me to question my path. In the moment, I made a choice and took an action that I knew would change my destiny; yet, I did it anyway. I hoped that my company would understand my choice and maybe even back me. That wasn't the case. I guess in that moment, I did feel betrayed. Fortunately, I was able to take that feeling, motivate myself, and turn it into something very positive — a new direction that fulfills me on a daily basis in ways that I never imagined possible. If I can do that in my professional life, why can't I do it in my personal life? I like to believe that I can.

In my personal life, I sometimes think about the energy of mutual romantic love. I realize that, as you get older, this energy visits you less and less. Symbolically, I look at mutual romantic love like trying to hold a handstand in yoga. I can stay up for about thirty seconds, but then I lose my way. With romantic love, you learn to see it in more of a temporary and sometimes momentary way. This hurts you. It feels within your grasp, but then you discover that it is not really available to you or you can't return the emotion in a mutual way. You begin to lose your desire to want it because it hurts so much when you think that you have it, but then discover that you don't. You feel like you're being mocked. That love is for others, not you. You need to stay motivated when it comes to love. True romantic love is a gift. It is a rare visitor. So when it appears, you have to value it and nurture it and not take it for granted. If you want love to stay, you have to do the work, part of which is to love yourself first.

How do you undo the effects of betrayal, rejection, and failure so that you can clear out the cloudiness and move on to achieve your goals — both professional and personal — without reliving past consequences? You learn to utilize the wound and embrace it instead of bury it and suppress it. You forgive. You move forward. You do the emotional work to process the disappointment, the heartbreak, and any other unresolved emotions. You meditate on what you want. You believe that it is possible. You process and heal from the past instead of escaping from it through a series of escapes and addictions. You create goals. You write life summary lines and story arcs that act as the roadmap to those goals. You take it one step at a time. You create a new path. You write your story the way you want it to materialize. You become the active hero in your story. You actively pursue your possibility.

As one author put it, all good stories begin "when an undeserved misfortune happens to the central character." So think about your story starting where this happened to you. Take your "undeserved misfortune" and utilize it to find the motivation to move forward and write a new story. First you have to understand why you made the choices that led you down a certain path in the first place. You have to really take inventory and understand why you made those choices, what effects those choices had on your spirit, and how you can make better choices in the future, coming from a stronger place of wisdom. This really does apply to both personal and professional loss. When you take the time to mend, you take the time to go within. When you go within, you take care of yourself and come to recognize that all the answers you're seeking on the outside are found within. As nearly every hero comes to realize, your real motivation comes from within. It is worth the time to go there and just *be*. Only then will you truly be ready to bring a new relationship into your life.

When you enter into a new relationship, you have to be ready to see a reflection of yourself through another person's perspective again. When you enter a new situation too early, you carry your unresolved conflict and integrate it into the new situation. You repeat past mistakes instead of learning from them. At this point, you often attract similar energy, people who have not taken the proper time to heal. You cling to one another believing that your raw wounds are connecting you, but you do not see that those wounds need to be fully healed before you are ready to connect again. In order to be ready for this, you should be completely happy with your own perspective of yourself before you are ready to take on another. Some people are never ready to connect again on a romantic level, and this is all right — your connection with self is more important.

Both my grandmother and my mother chose not to have serious relationships after their marriages ended. My grandmother, God rest her soul, had fourteen kids with my grandfather before he passed away at the young age of 62. As a child, I saw how this damaged my grandmother, my mother, and the rest of her family. My grandfather was taken too soon. The life lesson here is that when you break, sometimes there isn't a fix to what is broken. You move forward because that is what you must do, but you don't forget. I watched my mother go through the loss of her father at far too young an age — only 38 — and I will forever remember this. I know that in that moment, a part of her broke. She came home from the funeral and moved forward with her life. She went back to law school at 39 and became a lawyer. She found a new path; it was time to follow her own direction. My mother divorced my father after 27 years of marriage. She had a couple of relationships after the divorce, but nothing serious. She was the second of fourteen kids, married my dad at age 21, and had three kids by the time she was 27. So a part of me really does understand that she's been taking care of others all of her life. Now it's her time. I admire this. Time to "just be" is a gift. Taking care of you is a gift you give not only to yourself but to others as well, because you bring greater joy to those around you when you are happy within. Learning to connect with self on a level that empowers inner peace and contentment, and loving this companionship, is an attainable goal. You just have to do the emotional work to get to this place.

I remember a line in an episode of the BBC series *Luther*. The scene is between John Luther (Idris Elba) and Jane, a young girl Luther is helping. Jane says, "You're so nice. Why aren't you married? You should be married." Luther responds, "Because no one will have me." If you know the story, you understand why this line hits you in the heart. This line made my eyes well up. It showed such vulnerability in a very strong character. It is a line that represents how a lot of single people feel deep down and yet it is also a defense mechanism. If you stay behind the shroud and don't let anyone in, then you make the choice to be alone.

If being active in your personal life is something you desire, and you have a goal that you'd like to pursue in this area of your life, then we will go on this journey together. As I learn to apply some of the ambition I've shown in my professional life to my personal life, I will pass on what I learn. It is a scary endeavor. If you're like me, you find professional pursuits much safer than personal or emotional ones. Yet you deserve to be loved and to know what true love is on a romantic level, if this is what you desire. It all comes down to where your heart and spirit are and what pursuits fulfill your possibility.

Professionally, my life goals were motivated by my desire to do what I loved for a living. I knew that I loved stories. I knew this from a very young age. Stories warmed me up and comforted me when I was feeling down. Stories made me believe. Stories opened me up to the idea that I could create my own story. I come from a family of professionals. My father is a doctor. My mother is a lawyer. My sister is a lawyer who was just made a partner at her law firm, and my brother is a dentist who has his own practice. So I knew that in order for me to achieve, I had to learn how to find success with story development. This led me to study cinema at USC. I then found internships in the entertainment industry and worked in a few different areas before landing a job in producer Aaron Spelling's office. Aaron was my guardian angel. He helped me to believe in my talent through mentoring my vision on story. He was a perfectionist, so it didn't mean that it was always an easy place to learn; however, it was a place where there was constant growth and movement in the direction of my dream. After he died, I lost a very important person in my life. I had to learn to take the tools that he gave me and to move forward with my own story.

My contract was not picked up after fifteen years with the same company. So, what did I do to stay motivated? I started my own company, Jen Grisanti Consultancy Inc. What did I draw from? I drew from my love of stories. What was the wound that was driving me? The residual scar left from the experience, the fear that if I didn't go out on my own, the loss could happen all over again at a different company. Also, I didn't want to move backward with my life. I wanted to move forward. I felt that if I worked for someone else again, I was losing control of my destiny. I had worked very hard since college — seventeen years at that point. I knew that my experience and reputation had value. I knew that I had been mentored by the best. I knew that I had a message to deliver.

What were the flaws that got in my way? I would say that impatience was one of my flaws. Patience has definitely never been one of my greatest virtues. I knew where I wanted to go. I had just been on a fifteen-year climb toward owning the title of "Vice President." Now I had to start from scratch and build in a new direction. I would say that another flaw was expecting too much from myself too soon. Now, I would say that my flaw also encouraged my forward movement as well. When I saw my limitations in certain areas, I would buy a ton of books on whatever it was and I ended up learning so much through the lessons of others. What did I learn during my transformation? It's all about the journey and less about the destination. We have to keep our eye on the destination so that we know that we're moving forward; however, we have to learn to be present in the practice of creating the dream.

I mentioned earlier that external stakes are a part of what motivates the central character in all stories. The external stakes for me were that I had to figure out a way to create a living that would support my lifestyle, or else I could lose everything I had built. When I was younger, I remember hearing that most adults are three paychecks away from being homeless. Clearly, thoughts of this influenced my motivation. Truthfully, I was blessed to have the security of knowing that my parents would always open their doors to me. However, I also knew that they had given me the tools and the education to succeed, and that now it was up to me to take hold of all these strengths and apply them. The external stakes at this time for me did represent a metaphorical kind of death. So I used this to motivate me forward.

My company celebrated its five-year anniversary in January of 2013. It is growing at an enormous rate. They say that 95% of small businesses don't make it to year five. I give tremendous gratitude for understanding the elements of story and how to use my wounds, my flaws, and the external stakes to motivate the goal in my own story.

In your story, learning how to respond from the spirit and move forward in pursuit of fulfillment on a more authentic level is a worthwhile endeavor. It all comes down to motivation and identifying your external goal. What does the light at the end of the tunnel represent to you? What are you willing to do in order to get there? Take the time to answer these questions, as an investment in your future. Be in this process of writing your story, because it is a precious and priceless process. I believe that as long as you are alive and breathing, you can motivate yourself to pursue a goal, be it personal or professional. It is never too late. You just have to believe in the possibility of you. I believe in you. I know that if you put your mind and your heart to it, visualize it and meditate on it, anything is possible. When you write your story, you will better understand how to tell and sell your story. When you know how to do this, your opportunities will be limitless.

Exercise Two

Starting from the personal turning point that you chose in Exercise One, identify the external goal you will be traveling toward in your new story.

CHAPTER THREE

INITIAL GOALS, NEW GOALS

A hero is someone who has given his or her life to something bigger than oneself.
— *JOSEPH CAMPBELL*

WHEN YOU WERE YOUNG, WHAT DID YOU WANT TO BE WHEN YOU GREW up? I knew I wanted be in the entertainment business from an early age. As a child, I would get lost in stories. I watched TV shows like *The Brady Bunch* and *The Hardy Boys* and imagined what it would be like to tell stories for shows like these. It was my way of escaping. I knew that I wanted to be involved in storytelling in some way. My goal coming out of college was to decide which area of entertainment I wanted to pursue. Once I landed a job with Aaron Spelling's company, my world opened up. Through the scripts I read I discovered the power of words and messages. I found my heart in my work. From the time I was an assistant my goal was to someday run a studio. I could see how my climb up the corporate ladder could contribute to this outcome. When things changed, I took the time to create a new strategy. I made a new goal. My goal now involves expanding beyond the entertainment industry and teaching people in business how to tell and position their story in a way that will help them reach their bottom line and connect with their clients or customers on a higher level. My overall mission now is to stop isolation and create community on a global level through the revelation of our personal stories. I took what I loved as a child and I let it evolve into something much bigger. You can do the same.

In well-written fiction, a hero's goals change as he evolves throughout the course of the story. The initial goals he sets as a result of his turning point are not the more meaningful and fulfilling goals he ultimately arrives at, because he himself has changed for the better along his journey. When looking at your goals, think about how they have evolved or are evolving. What do you seek to feel internally and externally from the achievement of your goal? How are you going to move from ego to spirit in the process? You can draw from your initial dream. How can you link what you dreamed about *then* to what you want *now*? You can grow your dream from the seed that it was into a revitalized dream that will not only help you, but also contribute to the greater good.

There are four things I want you to consider when thinking about your life goals:

- Internal and external
- Creating change
- Moving from ego to spirit
- Evolving toward the greater good

Internal and External

By looking at your initial life goals and understanding why you wanted what you wanted, you can learn to use that information in formulating your present goals and setting your future goals. Think back to when you were young and innocent, and try to recall a time when you had no reason to believe that your dreams couldn't come true. You lived inside your imagination, where anything was possible, and you thought that when the time came the world would be at your fingertips. Then life happened. You went in pursuit of your dreams. Maybe the pursuit brought the dream to life, or perhaps the dream wasn't quite like what you initially imagined. Or maybe you never did fully attain what you thought was your initial plan. Whether you attained the goals or not, often the feeling at the finish line wasn't what you thought it would be. You pursued your goals because you understood what you wanted. However, you may not have given a lot of thought to *why* you wanted it.

By aligning what you want with why you want it, you will discover a greater sense of inner peace at the outcome. These pursuits refer to both the personal and the professional goals in your life. By looking back at why you wanted what you wanted when you were young, you can now better understand your motivations behind the dream. By doing this, it will help you to define why you want what you want *now*. As you evolve through life and begin to see the value of moving from ego to spirit, you begin to recognize that the pursuit of your goals can be about more than just self-satisfaction; it can be about helping the greater good. When your motivation to achieve your goals goes to a deeper level, you add strength to your emotional drive for the goal. This adds fuel to your pursuit because it comes from the inside out.

What were your initial goals when you graduated from high school or college? Which of them have you attained? Were your accomplishments professional or personal? What did the road toward these accomplishments look like? What obstacles did you hit along the way? By looking at what your initial goals were, what you attained, what you still want to attain, and what you felt as a result of the accomplishment, you will begin to see what you've learned and how you can apply it toward your new goals. To create change in your story, look at your falls and rejections with new perspective. See them as an opportunity to know what tactics didn't work. Think of all the goals you have accomplished. For each accomplishment you've achieved, you've gathered tools that have helped you to move toward your next accomplishment. You've gained confidence and belief from your past achievements by experiencing first-hand that you can do it. Utilize the positive emotions you've felt from past achievements, when you are planning your current life goals.

In this chapter I want you to go back in time and tap into the emotions that motivated your initial goals. If you did achieve some or all of these goals, did you feel these emotions in the outcome? Did these emotions feel like they were linked up to the right goal? By looking at this, you will see a blueprint from your past that can inform how you will write your story now. Look at the following statements and take note of how many you have said yourself: When I meet the right person I will know what true happiness is; When I get married my life will be complete; When I have a child I will understand what unconditional love is; When I get promoted to VP I will feel validated; When I buy a big home I will feel that I've attained my "happily ever after"; when I have financial freedom I will feel that I've succeeded. And the list goes on. You can get stuck trying to fulfill this list because maybe you have the wrong emotional expectations connected to these outcomes. Just as a character in fiction re-evaluates and evolves for the better, as you evolve your goals come from a deep place inside yourself. The answers to everything you want to feel on the outside lie within. You just need to learn how to do the work to connect with your authentic self so that your external goals can better reflect your internal motivations and expectations.

At the beginning of your life, it is natural that most of the goals you want to achieve are for self-motivated reasons. You want to prove that you can do it. You want to shine in your parents' eyes. You want to feel validated. You want to feel loved. You want to have things that maybe reflect to others that you have succeeded. As you get older, when you look at your pursuits and achievements you often end up feeling that the outcome wasn't quite in alignment with the internal part of your dream. You thought that if your dreams came true, even part of them, there would be all of these splendid emotions that would fill your life. You would feel complete. When you reached your goal, you didn't feel the sense of completeness that you thought would accompany your achievement. So maybe what you thought you wanted for internal reasons wasn't really what you truly wanted in your heart. You often have to get to the destination to discover this.

By examining the external (what you want) and the internal (why you want it) aspects of your goals, you will begin to see your patterns. Are your patterns working for you or against you? Is your philosophy faulty? What went into the creation of your patterns? You may want to consider really looking at them and then, if need be, you can make changes. In fiction, the central character often begins the story with a faulty philosophy. It is through the journey of the story that he begins to wake up and see that his philosophy is no longer working for him. This is why I want you to look at your past and your patterns so that you can see if your philosophy was part of what was holding you back then. It will help you to see what your philosophy is doing to you now. Understanding this will help you with the construction of your new story.

Creating Change

Moving out of your comfort zone will be part of the transformation that I wish for you in reading this book. Transformation is something that takes time. By looking at the motivations behind the attainment of your goals, and learning to change the motivations and your attachment to the outcome of your goals, you can change your story. I've learned in life that to attain a goal of great value you have to be willing to put in the work that it takes to get there. You have to see the beauty in the journey, not just the destination. The destination is what you want to reach. However, don't be blind to what you learn along the way. The tools that you learn on your journey to one destination will be the ones you reach for when you set a new goal after attaining the last one. I will show you how to do some of the work by guiding you to put a plan in place that will lead to your change.

I try to practice meditation on a daily basis. When I first wake up in the morning, I meditate for fifteen minutes. During this time, I think about all of my immediate goals, both work-related and personal. Although, let's be honest, most of what I meditate on are my professional goals because this is where I feel safe. Through the process of writing this book, my goal is to meditate more on getting results in my personal life every bit as much as the professional. When I meditate, I visualize everything I want to materialize with the goal. I see it happening. I revel in the feeling of the achievement. I believe in the outcome. I fuel the idea that there is no limit. I know that where there's a will, there's a way, and that I can make it happen. For inspiration I review my history and think back to the first day of every goal that I set for myself. Who was I on that first day of the goal? Who have I become in the process of achieving it? Do I like the person who I've become in the process of the goal? If not, could I? The achievement of the goal can bring out the best in a person and it can also bring out the worst. It all comes down to your motivation. Why do you want to achieve this goal? Is it connected to pride and ego? Or is it connected to spirit? As we change, our motivation for why we want what we want changes. It's up to you to be motivated by the things that are genuine and true to you in the attainment of your goal. In order to do this, you must have a stronger understanding of everything on an internal, external, and spiritual level that is going into the end result.

A great way to get into the practice of meditation is to do the 21-Day Meditation Challenge with Deepak Chopra. I highly recommend it. They say that it takes 21 days to change and create a new habit or to move through change when something happens. I find that this challenge made my meditation practice even more consistent. I loved going through the guided meditation; it helped me to reflect on my life and what I want in an even deeper way than doing it on my own. I really looked forward to hearing what the message was each day and taking the time to reflect on it and absorb it. I realize that when we do the work to create change, change happens.

One of the guided meditations by Deepak Chopra that I connected with focused on three words: "Open to love." As I meditated on these words, I thought of all the people who, like me, have hearts that have shut down in some way due to choices, fear, past wounds, and just our inability to trust ourselves. We get clogged and our heart suffers. Our hearts shutting down can happen when we are single or when we are married. I meditated on the idea of clearing what is clogging my heart. I thought back to a time when I felt true romance and viewed it as a gift. I viewed love in a particular way. I believed in its possibility. I allowed myself to dream big. I thought that I was clear on the kind of love that I wanted to attract. While I've experienced shades of love attached to a preconceived notion and expectation that may have been flawed on my side, I feel ready to experience love in a new way with a new hope in my heart for something that has evolved on a much deeper level. I want this for all of us who know what it's like to close off, shut down, and become clogged.

This reminds me of a line from a movie that resonated with me on a deep level. In the film *Up in the Air*, written by Jason Reitman from the novel by Walter Kirn, Natalie (Anna Kendrick) says to Ryan (George Clooney), "You put yourself in a cocoon of self-banishment." Just as this shocked the character in the story, I think it woke up many of those who watched the film. She was shining a light on the fact that the philosophy on love that he'd been clinging to was not working for him. Ryan's philosophy portrayed at the beginning of the film had to do with going through life with only a light backpack. The backpack symbolized being detached from commitments. In the beginning of the story, we see how Ryan's attachment to this philosophy is what is holding him back. We watch as he transforms through the story after hitting obstacles, and in this moment when Natalie shines the light on him, he begins to take action toward changing his philosophy. If you want your story to have romance, you have to do the internal work and make space for the possibility.

Your body is another area in which you may want to create change and set goals. You may want to be thinner. You may want to achieve more muscle definition. You may want to just feel better about the choices you make when it comes to food. I think that your body is a great way to see what setting goals can do. You do have control over what you eat. When you eat healthy and get regular exercise, you see results. When you see results, it adds to your being motivated. When you create change from the inside out, you see that your story can change simply by the choices you make.

Having a healthy mind, spirit, and body are at the foundation of any change you can make in your life. When you take the time to learn about how to breathe, how to be in the present, and how what you eat can change your life, you empower your own possibility. I believe that yoga is another thing that has changed my life. I have practiced yoga for around eighteen years now. I've become very dedicated to my yoga practice in the last ten years. I love it because it is an activity that fuels my body, mind, and spirit. This means that I am working out at a stronger level because it involves going to a deep place inside. Meditation, healthy eating, and yoga are all three excellent ways to set your foundation for change.

Moving from Ego to Spirit

Going from ego to spirit in your life and in your story is characterized by the shift from external rewards to internal rewards. Both have merit. I would say that you are in a struggle between the ego and the spirit on a daily basis. You can be fueled by both, just understand the balance. The ego can be utilized in a beneficial way. It's just learning when to listen to it and when to turn it off. As I get older, I am finding that the hunger of my spirit being fulfilled is outweighing the desire of my ego; however, I recognize that I had to go through my ego being satiated to get to a place where the spirit fulfillment means more. As you begin to connect more with your spirit on your journey, you evolve into a higher sense of your purpose. You think about how the attainment of your goals can contribute to the betterment of others. Perhaps it extends even beyond the betterment of others and becomes about how you can effect change on a global (limitless) scale. You must take the time to understand the message that comes through you and know how to deliver it. Give gratitude for the gift of coming into your higher purpose. You are on your own journey. You are exactly where you are supposed to be. You create your story. If change is something that you want, you have the ability to make it happen.

I have a plaque on my desk given to me by my close friend Noelle, who overcame cancer. On the plaque is a quote from Gandhi: "Be the change you wish to see in the world." I think about this every morning as I set out on my daily goals. How can the goals that I set for myself affect others and contribute to the change that I wish to see in the world? By owning my own business, which helps others achieve their dreams through writing, I know that I am, in my own small way, contributing to the greater good. By guiding writers to go within for answers when sharing their stories, I am empowering the use of their voices. Your voice appears when you learn to draw from within. Sharing your story is the way you connect with others. Your truth is part of this. You have to be ready to go within, seek your truth, and communicate it openly. When you do this, your world will open up in ways that you never imagined.

Having an awareness of how you feel during your moments of ego gratification might help you determine if you are ready to move from your ego to your spirit. Are you happy in these moments? Does a part of you feel unfulfilled? I'll share my experience as a way of illustrating this point. When I worked at the studio as a Current Programs executive, I found that the way I measured my success was by how many shows were returning to the broadcast schedule. Current Programming is the department that a TV show goes to after moving through Development and being picked up from a pilot to a series. Our job was to work on the show from concept to screen and everything in between. So, when the shows succeeded, it reflected well on everyone involved. You could measure the success in your bonus and in the raises that you got each year. While I was in this hierarchy of achievement, I fed off of it. I put my heart into every show that I worked on. I wanted to be the best at what I did. I wanted to receive the big bonuses, the shiny perks, and the validation from my peers. These were some of the external and internal rewards that motivated my achievement. For a time, these rewards served a tremendous purpose for my growth as a person. Externally, they helped confirm that I was achieving my "happily ever after" experience. Internally, I was beginning to question their value in connection with my path.

I remember certain moments during these achievements. Some were incredible highs while others were low and strewn with deep contemplation. My ego and my spirit were cognizant during my journey, but at this time in my life, my ego was devouring more time. My ego loved being seen out at ritzy restaurants with top people in the business. My spirit starved for true connection in some of these moments. My ego loved that my achievement came with a title, a big office, an assistant, and a bonus. My spirit struggled with the idea that the attainment of all of this often resulted at a spiritual cost. When you are in these types of positions, the workload can be endless. You become addicted to the work because, in doing the work, you see the achievement. I had so much to do that somewhere along the way I became numb and I lost connection with myself. As a result, I was losing the ability to connect with others — I mean *truly* connect. Now, I see lots of others in business go through this same lack of attention to the moment. The iPhone is on the table. There are constant interruptions. The opportunity to truly connect becomes shaded by the perception of importance. Back then, during some of these moments of deep contemplation, I would ask myself: Who am I becoming in the attainment of this dream? Do I like this person? Am I happy in this pursuit? In hindsight, I look back at this and wonder what I was trying to prove. Was it that I was so important that I couldn't share a meal without being needed by someone? What was this all about?

These questions helped me to see that my ego had been satiated but that my spirit was still starved. I had my piece of the pie, but it wasn't enough to satisfy me on the inside. I loved the creative process of working on the shows and watching them succeed. I loved the process of working with the writers. I knew that I was good at my job because of the results I saw on the screen and because of the fact that I had so many shows returning. However, when I was at the studio, I felt somewhat limited by the studio/network perspective with regard to how far we could go with any story. Everyone had to adhere to this. Creatively there was a part of me that yearned to be closer to the creative process by having more freedom. Even though I never anticipated it happening the way that it did, perhaps my energy manifested the push in a new direction that I received.

After finding out that the studio was not going to renew my contract, I went through so many emotions. It's difficult to even describe the experience because a lot of the emotions contrasted one another. I was terrified to lose the security. I was joyous to be free. I was shocked to hear that after one moment where I sided with my value system, it was over. I was thrilled that I was going to be paid until the end of my contract. I was devastated that my identity was so tied to my position. I was excited at the possibility of building a new identity. I was scared that everything I had worked for was vanishing when the job disappeared. As I went further into processing this change, I was wondering if I had connected the right rewards to the goal. My rewards were so ego-driven, so external. I couldn't see that before, but I can see it now. It was time to create some new goals in my life that grew from a deep internal and spiritual place. I was ready. I wanted something deeper. I wanted what I did for others to mean more to them and to me.

And here is something amazing. When we learn to go within for validation, we begin to see that there is no limit to what we can accomplish and create. We don't have someone setting boundaries and telling us we can't. We shift into the idea of possibility and saying that we can. We move into understanding the emotional fulfillment of the outcome.

We learn to see the ego in the light, embrace what it brought and move through it to a deeper place. We process. We struggle. We face obstacles. We overcome the obstacles. We shed. We let go. We transform.

Part of what I did to change my story was to really look at what I loved about what I did in my job. Where were my strengths? How could I find a direction that capitalized on them? I realized that my strength had always been my development notes. On my last phone call with Aaron Spelling, he told me that he had said to Les Moonves, the head of CBS/Paramount, that I gave the best story notes of any development executive out there. This was the last call that I had with Aaron before he died. I remember his words because they are what I turned to after losing my job. Part of taking the promotion to VP at CBS/Paramount meant losing the alliance I had known my whole career with Aaron Spelling. I remember the strength of his words on our last call. He was saying goodbye to me in the capacity that he had known me: as an executive who rose through the ranks of his company due to his mentoring and belief in my talent, and he was encouraging me to embrace and believe in my new direction through reminding me about his belief in me. It was the greatest gift he gave me, a gift that no one will ever be able to take from me. It was this gift that fueled my recognition of where my strength lived — in my story notes. This is what contributed to the birth of my company, a writers' consultancy designed to help writers reach writing goals and career destinations. I knew that I wanted to build a company that was all about the favorite part of my job and that capitalized on my strength. I also knew that by creating a company like this, I was going to help others achieve their dreams. My focus was moving from the external to the internal motivations behind my goal. By understanding this, I created my niche.

Sometimes it takes the belief of others to help you see what you are truly capable of achieving. For me, Aaron Spelling's belief in me was a very large part of what fueled me. It helped me to believe in myself. When you combine your parents' belief in your path with the confidence mentors have instilled in you along the way, you can tap into your own belief in yourself and build and nurture it by creating the results you want to see in your life based on your own values and ethics versus the values of others. Now, you may not have the blessing of a positive mentor to draw from, be it a boss, a teacher, or a parent. Does this mean that you can't achieve your goals? It absolutely does not. I think if you haven't had positive role models in your life who've helped you believe in your possibility, you just have to do the emotional work to learn to bring this to yourself without it having to be channeled through others. How often have we seen a hero in a movie standing alone as he faces his final challenge? You can be the person who believes in you without any outside influence.

You create your own vision. You connect from within and learn to attach the right motivations to your end goal. You evolve from past rejections, hurt, and perceived failure. You move from the ego to the spirit. You begin to see things more clearly. You learn to look within. You formulate a plan and put it into action. You find your niche. This is the best part of being an entrepreneur: shepherding your vision, doing it on your own terms, knowing that there is no one telling you that you can't do something, and feeling that your direction is limitless. There is no competition other than competing with yourself to be the best you can be. There is no greater high than seeing and believing in your own ability to accomplish and change your story so that your new direction is one that follows your spirit.

Evolving Into the Greater Good

I've discussed the concepts of internal versus external and of moving from ego to spirit. Now I'd like to talk about a divinely inspired drive for your goals to benefit the greater good. As you evolve through life, you move into a higher state of consciousness and your motivation for why you want what you want changes. As you move into this greater consciousness, you begin to connect with the spiritual part of your goals. You see that if you redefine the internal motivation or drive, then it could change the external part of your goal. In making these changes, you could move into an even deeper part of the goal, driven by your higher purpose or the greater good. When you think about the greater good, imagine a limitless space where what you do can affect the masses in a very big way. When you move into this higher consciousness, you return to innocence, but with a renewed sense of wisdom. You now know that your pursuit isn't as fulfilling when it's just about you. Your pursuits will be even more fulfilling if you determine how they can benefit the greater good in the message that you send out.

Finding this kind of success that is motivated from within and not only helps you but also contributes to the greater good is like falling in love. I have been in love a few times. I remember when I was in the grip of love, I wanted everyone to feel what I was feeling and know happiness at the extreme level that I was experiencing it. I would say when you come into your own voice as an entrepreneur you go through the same type of extreme emotion. You want everyone around you to understand how to use their turning points to change their story and transform their potential. Sometimes it takes hitting rock bottom and going into the depth of darkness to help you to see and appreciate the light. You move through it. You become empowered. You want others to see that there is no limit to what can be accomplished. When you have a dream and you see it clearly and you see the achievement of it, you can make it happen. This is why daily meditation and visualizing the achievement of the goal helps so much. Professionally, I am always picturing the positive outcome of the goals that I set and, as a result, they are happening. My achievements are no longer just about me, they are about serving others and benefitting the greater good in the process. If I can do it, I know that you can do it too.

How do you find your professional niche? You look at your strengths. What are some of your strengths? Think about what people have told you all your life from the time you were a child. What are some of the qualities that teachers pointed out to you? What are some moments you can recall where you really felt you were great at something? Did you nurture that gift? If not, can you go back to it and nurture it now? Write down a list of your strengths. Now consider the market. Is there a market or a demand that you envision your strengths filling? Is there a niche that could capitalize on your strengths? I bet there is.

By going to the positive part of your growth, you see and breathe your new possibility. The work is in letting go of the negative experiences and choosing to use them to fuel you instead of allowing them to weigh you down. It is your choice. If you want to create and change your story, you need to know what you want your story to be. You also need to be ready for the change.

Change comes down to coming up with a winning strategy. When you think about your end goal and how it is connected to the greater good, you draw up a plan to get there. You carefully build that plan. You think about the motivations and where they come from with regard to making it happen. Are they limited to the external rewards? Could you think more about the internal and the spiritual components? How can you learn to utilize them? You think about how you can attach your end goal to spiritual reasons versus ego. You learn how to move forward. You will no doubt hit some obstacles along the way; however, when you start to view these obstacles as growth opportunities versus setbacks, you will see that there is tremendous value in learning how to get over them.

Learning how to connect the internal (your motivations and emotions) to the external (your goals and rewards) will be part of your journey in changing your story. It's all about learning how you can feel truly fulfilled internally through achieving externally. In order to do this, you have to do the work to better understand what it is that you want internally. When you move from the external rewards to the internal rewards, you grow and connect more with your spirit. When you look at your own motivations and explore why you want what you want, you will find your answers. Looking at your goals from every angle will help you make changes. Understanding what was and is ego-motivated, and knowing that there is something more rewarding, will drive you toward creating a new destiny and changing your story. There is no limit to what your story can be.

Exercise Three

Utilizing the turning point you chose in Exercise One and the external goal you identified in Exercise Two, write your "life summary line" and "story arc" for your new story. Think back on the arcs of your initial life goals for inspiration.

The formula for your "life summary line" is:

- Set-up of "who"
  (present the protagonist and their strengths/weaknesses)
- Dilemma
- Action
- Goal

Components of your story arc are:

1. Starting dilemma
2. External goal stemming from dilemma
3. Thematic question
4. Actions taken
5. Obstacles hit leading up to your "all is lost" moment
6. External and/or internal stakes
7. Attainment of your goal

CHAPTER FOUR

DILEMMAS

HOW DO PAST WOUNDS INFLUENCE WHICH CHOICES YOU MAKE?

As the builders say, the larger stones do not lie well without the lesser.
— PLATO

WHEN I WOKE UP THE DAY AFTER MY JOB AS A STUDIO EXECUTIVE ended, I knew that I was facing the biggest choice of my life. What did I want to do next? Was I going to go the safe route and get another corporate job with a big company? Was I going to continue my climb up the corporate ladder? Did losing my job mean I was losing some rungs on the ladder? Could I regain what I had lost? Was I ready to go out on my own? Did I have what it takes to shepherd my own vision? Had I learned enough from my mentors to do it alone or would I be jumping off the biggest cliff of my career up to now? These are some of the questions I faced in my dilemma. Dilemmas reveal character. When we are pushed between a rock and a hard place, and a choice has to be made, our choice is what will lead us in a new direction. Our new direction stems from the external goal that we choose as a result of facing our dilemma.

In your life you often hit moments when you have to make a choice about which direction you want to go. Metaphorically speaking, you hit a fork in the road and must decide which direction will lead you down the strongest path and move you closer toward your life's purpose. Having to choose between two directions is a dilemma. By making a choice you become an active hero in your life. Dilemmas are opportunities for you to define what you want. What exactly is a dilemma? As Wikipedia defines it, "A dilemma is a situation or problem offering two options where neither choice is easy or definitively clear." In retrospect, you may think that some of your past dilemmas led you in the wrong direction. The truth is, any direction that you go in is the right direction because it is part of your life's journey. There is always something you are supposed to learn from every choice you make. Even if the choice leads to a negative experience, it is part of your growth. You can learn how to use the choices you've made when faced with past dilemmas to inform the choices you make when faced with a new dilemma. If you begin to see any dilemma you face as the starting point of your story and a trigger moment that leads you into action in the pursuit of a goal, you can turn your dilemma into something positive. Your darkest turning points, which happen as a result of your dilemmas, can lead you to your greatest successes.

In fiction, establishing a clear dilemma is a great way to start the story. By putting a central character between a rock and a hard place, a writer reveals a lot about their character through the choice the character makes. When the character makes a choice, ultimately, a goal will stem from this choice that helps them to move in what they hope is a stronger direction. The external goal defines what the character wants on a physical level. If done well, the choice made reveals a lot about the character's past wound or wounds. In doing this, the writer creates empathy for the character. In revealing the character's wounds, a writer begins to establish motivation. With motivation, we go into the internal reason behind the external goal. Why does the character want to achieve it? What emotions does the character hope to feel as a result of obtaining the external goal? Lastly, the writer wants to establish the stakes. What is the worst thing that can happen if the goal is not achieved? Ideally, you want to feel that not achieving the goal is associated with a sense of doom or either real or metaphorical death. This makes the audience feel and connect with the plight of the central character. When a writer starts with a dilemma, it forces their central character to make a choice at the beginning of their story, and gives us a sense of what is driving their central character. Then the writer creates empathy by illuminating the character's strengths and weaknesses, and gives us a reason to root for the goal being achieved. You can learn to mimic this process and apply it to your own life. Write your story from a place that utilizes these creative tools to help get you to where you want to go. Create the story that you want your life to reflect.

An example of a strong dilemma in a story is perfectly illustrated in the film *The King's Speech*. We learn that our central character, "Bertie" (Colin Firth), the younger son of King George V, has a tremendous fear of speaking in public. We discover this as he's about to give his first public speech and, in front of everyone including his father and older brother, he stutters heavily throughout. His worst fear is realized. His secret is out. It is revealed that he has a profound stutter. We see Bertie put himself down because of his limitations. We empathize with him, knowing that giving speeches is part of his royal responsibility. We understand the stakes: If he doesn't get over his stutter, he may never be the leader his father was. He would fail himself and his family. This would lead to a kind of metaphorical death. In the beginning, Bertie is protected from this happening because it falls on his older brother to step up to the throne as King after their father dies. Then there is a major turning point when his brother steps down from the throne to marry a divorced woman. Bertie is forced to step up as he is crowned King George VI. This major turning point prompts Bertie to change. This escalates the stakes for Bertie to learn to get over his stutter. His dilemma now has the attention of the nation tied to it. If he does nothing to improve his stutter, the people of England will view him as a failure. If he does the work to move past his stutter, he could be a tremendous leader during a time of war. This is a great dilemma. What's at stake? Internally, he could gain the respect, dignity, and validation that he has been seeking all of his life. Externally, he could fill his father's shoes and lead the nation from a place of power.

The choices you make as a result of the dilemmas that you face following your turning points reveal a lot about your character. In life, on average, you will experience half a dozen major turning points that influence your life story. These turning points may include marriage, the birth of a child, a divorce, a career change, the death of a loved one, an illness or impairment, etc. These turning points, and the wounds and scars that result from them, influence a majority of the choices we make. Some of your major turning points come from decisions you've made, while others result from the decisions others have made for which you are left to pick up the pieces (a little later I will share with you a story that reflects this type of experience). It is wild to think about life's turning points and how these experiences can determine so much. In these turns you find some of your deepest scars, but also some of your strongest motivations to move forward. You can learn to see your turning points and all of your dilemmas as opportunities to be more decisive and to help you to weigh the costs and rewards of moving in any given direction. Your turning points and dilemmas lead you to make a choice about your external goal. When you set an external goal, you become an active hero in your life story. By this point, if you have done the exercises, you have identified the external goal in your new story and started to develop your story arc. It all stems from your starting dilemma.

Our dilemmas start when we are quite young. Think about how you viewed things such as your appearance and your weight when you were growing up. I remember that my weight became an issue after I was in an accident and the medication I took led to some weight gain. I was ten years old, and I had been thin up to that point. The trigger moment came when a boy who I had a crush on at school told me that

I had gotten fat. I will never forget this moment. Gaining the weight, the humiliation I felt by his comment, and other things going on in my life at the time, led to an eating disorder that lasted on and off from the age of 12 to 22. At my lowest point, I weighed 86 pounds. When you recover from bulimia and anorexia, you gain clarity, and you see that there is nothing good that comes from it. Yet when you are in the midst of the eating disorder, you can't see this. This is the dilemma I faced with my weight — if I keep doing what I am doing, I will hurt my body to the point that I could die; however, if I can motivate myself to heal my body and mind, and move past this, I will have a happier life. At age 22, I stopped. I didn't seek help. I knew intellectually that I had it in me to move past this. I was ready to change. If anyone had approached me about it when I wasn't ready, I would not have been able to do it. The cost was too great on one side and the reward of learning how to eat a balanced diet and exercise in a healthy way was something I knew I could do. So by weighing both sides of the dilemma I learned that even though one side involved more work, it also involved being healthy. Fortunately, I chose my health.

Earlier on I mentioned that I had a long relationship end in a short marriage. I'd like to talk about the dilemma of getting married in the first place. We are socialized to believe that marriage is what defines the "happily ever after" in our story. For this reason, many men and women marry for the wrong reasons. We experience love and think that marriage is the way to validate it. We desire to conform. We want to feel committed. We want to do what our parents did. We connect marriage with the idea of feeling whole. We want to experience our "happily ever after" moment, and we believe it will surely come with marriage. We do it because society leads us to believe that this is what we are supposed to do. We're afraid that if we don't get married by a certain age, people will think no one wants us. We fear being alone for the rest of our lives. We believe that once we marry, we will gain security in the relationship that was missing before. We think that getting married means they won't leave. Maybe we marry because we want to have children. We believe that marriage is the only answer to our happiness instead of considering that there might be other alternatives.

I faced a dilemma when my now ex-husband proposed two years into our relationship. At the time, my career was just starting. He was a working actor and everything seemed to be falling into place. Our dreams seemed accessible. There were high points in our relationship where our dreams felt as if they were one. Then he went from two years of steady work to two years of unemployment. This brought about a change. To begin with, our backgrounds were very different on many levels. When we first met, I remember thinking that if this doesn't work it will be because our different backgrounds clashed. Yet, I didn't listen to that inner voice. I was young and believed love could conquer all. I remember having a moment in our relationship where everything in me knew that it wasn't right. I couldn't see our future together. I couldn't see growing old with this man. I wanted to see it, but I couldn't.

The dilemma I faced had to do with turning 30. This age can be a major turning point for women. At that point, I had put close to four years into this relationship. We had lived together for three of the four years. I knew that if I chose to listen to my instincts, I might never know what it's like to have my fairy tale ending and to have a child. Between this and being blinded by love and attraction, I decided not to listen to my gut, but instead to get married. I convinced myself that all people in relationships have problems and come from different backgrounds. If they could learn how to make it work, then I would learn to do the same. It was part of my life process. I knew that we had what I considered to be the most important ingredient: love. Looking back on how I viewed love then makes me see how differently I view it now. When we have love in the palm of our hands and we fail to nurture it in the best way possible and we lose it, we lose a part of ourselves in the process. I often wonder what my life would look like now had I chosen to follow my gut. Would my emotional wounds be as deep? Would I have met someone who was a better match for me? Despite these thoughts, I know this experience was part of my journey, so I have no regrets.

My second major life turn came with the loss of my job. The dilemma I faced was deciding whether to continue on the corporate route and wait for a good job offer to come along or to go out on my own and create my own company. After my job ended, I had nine months' salary in the bank. I knew from the experience of others going through similar situations that it could take one or two years before I'd find another great job that would utilize my skill set and be a step forward in my career. So there was a ticking clock on this decision. If I didn't find the ideal job in nine months, I would have to take something just to take it, which would be a step backward. I think that my wound from my divorce played into this fear as well as some past experiences at work that involved less than ideal situations. The idea of going out on my own was enthralling and terrifying at the same time. I had to really consider both sides. If I continued on the corporate route, I would continue down the road of security with my 401(k) and pension. I would be traveling the safer route, but at what cost to me on a personal level? During my career, I had faced some challenging circumstances with immediate bosses. The stress caused by these situations had taken a toll on my health. While these experiences made me stronger and contributed to my growth, they also taught me that I was ready to be my own boss. So the decision to start my own company seemed clear.

I knew the other side of the equation also had its obstacles. What if I went out on my own and I failed? To help me work through this, I read a ton of business books. I wanted to hear the stories of people who had done what I wanted to do. The common thread I found was that so many of these successful entrepreneurs had similar stories to mine. Many of them had either lost a major job, or had struggled dealing with irrational bosses, or had health issues resulting from doing something that wasn't in alignment with their value system. I realized that it was their story that motivated them to succeed. If they could use their own personal stories to drive them to greater success, I thought why not use my story to do the same? They were being driven by something greater. So, after doing a ton of research and seeking the advice of friends and former colleagues, I decided to take the chance and go out on my own.

As I mentioned earlier, in writing it's often said that a story begins when an undeserved misfortune happens to the central character. I knew that my story had this element, as well as other elements of story. When my job contract wasn't renewed, it was unexpected; no one in the community saw it coming, including me. In the beginning, the outpour of empathy was tremendous. This served a purpose for me. It helped me to see and value my worth. I was a known reader and my script notes were valued. I had helped staff more than fifteen shows in my career. I had played a role in launching several very big writing careers. I had established myself as someone who knew how to put a staff together. This meant something. This had value. So when I was out of a job, I became aware that a large amount of people empathized with my situation. Since I was in the midst of a transition and facing a powerful dilemma, I knew that this was where my new story was beginning.

The goal of this chapter is to help you see that although the turning points and dilemmas you face can be devastating in the moment, they can also catapult you in a stronger direction toward your true life's purpose. They are put in your path for a reason. They contribute to your growth and add to the message you pass forward. They can help you become more active in your life. Everything you experience in your life and the way you choose to interpret it is the gold in your story. How you choose to mine this experience determines the direction you will go in. The idea is to learn to be active after a fall versus falling victim to the experience. Take the time to process it, grieve it, understand it, and then use the tools you've gained from it to move you in a stronger direction.

Since I work with people's stories every day and am fascinated and inspired by them, I sent out a questionnaire to a select group of people asking about their major life turning points and dilemmas. I was astonished by how many fascinating stories I received back. I felt humbled by and grateful for the gift of the respondents' words, their willingness to be so open and so honest about their experiences. In most cases, I will fictionalize their names. For starters, I'd like to share with you a few of the startling turning points and dilemmas faced by some of the respondents of the questionnaire in order to demonstrate the variety of dilemmas encountered.

The first story comes from Howard and his son, Chad, who granted me permission to use their real names. This is what Howard had to say about his life turning point: "Definitely losing my eyesight at age 20 while on a search and destroy mission in the jungles of Vietnam. My world literally turned upside down within a matter of seconds. This one turning point was my most significant, and little did I know the impact it would have on me, as well as thousands of others."

Howard's second turning point shows the power of how he processed his pain and used it to move him in a more authentic direction: "Winning the Freshman Five Award, finishing #2 in the nation as a rookie agent with Mass Mutual Financial Group, winning the Oscar of Salesmanship, and sharing my story with Paul Harvey among 5,000 guests at Ford Theater in Detroit Michigan all within a few years of losing my eyesight. I finally began to feel like a man again."

Next, Howard's son, Chad, gave his account of his first major dilemma and turning point: "My birth. As I entered the physical world of sight, my father exited the physical world of sight and he had to discover a new world. This turned our family's life upside down for many years while he adjusted."

Their stories are powerful, compelling, and inspiring. Decisions they made as a result of their turning points have benefitted the masses in a major way. They moved through their egos into a spirit realm where they took action for the greater good. I will go deeper into their stories throughout the book because Howard and Chad are an outstanding example of people who used their turning points to move them in a more authentic direction.

I will refer to this next person as Anne. She had this to say about her life's dilemmas and turning points: "I was born to an angry, frightened alcoholic father and a clinically depressed mother, during a time when the world was not as enlightened as it is today. (No Oprah.) People hid their dirty laundry in closets and dealt only with what they were forced to at the time. Children had no rights and no voice. One of my earliest memories is lying in bed with my mother and sister. My father, who was drunk, sat in a chair by the bed with a shotgun, reminding us with slurred words that if we tried to run he'd shoot us all dead before we reached the door. I was five."

I have to say, I was so moved by Anne's raw honesty in the depiction of her life. She learned how to use her wounds to move forward. In her story, she was able to remove herself and see it in such a mature and detached way. This is the gift of a true writer.

I am sharing with you stories that reflect a broad spectrum of the turning points faced by real people. What you will find is that even though our stories are often very different, the emotions we experience as a result of these experiences are often very universal. It is what connects us to one another.

Many people are born into a turning point. The next story comes from Rosemary, who gives an account of what this life experience looks like: "My birth was a huge turning point for my parents, and as such, for me as well. I was their love child, the product of an eight-year affair. My mother left her husband and son in Seattle, Washington, and brought me to The Bronx, where we lived alone for three years while she waited for my dad to leave his wife of twenty-five years and five children. When he did finally leave his wife and kids, he came for us and brought us back west. My grandparents on both sides were dead set against our family, my aunts (mom's sisters) hated my dad, and all my older brothers and sisters wanted nothing to do with me. My parents' marriage was not the fairy tale mom thought it would be. My dad lost his job as a foreign diplomat because of his divorce, we had no money, mom worked three jobs to take care of us, dad's drinking went from bad to worse, mom and dad fought all the time, and then there was the abuse. I was born with my world upside down."

When your turning point starts with your birth, there is probably a greater challenge to face as you get older and begin to process the turning point that had nothing to do with you; it wasn't a dilemma you faced or a decision you made, but instead was a dilemma faced and a decision made by your parent(s) and you were left to face the consequences. It is in situations like the ones I've shared with you so far that we begin to truly find our spirit. For some, coming into your spirit takes longer because your first pivotal turn doesn't happen so early in life. For others, you come into the world connecting with your spirit from the beginning in order to draw strength from it to survive.

In your life, think of starting your new story with a dilemma you have faced or are facing now. What road do you want to travel? What have you learned from your past dilemmas and the choices you've made? Think about your past wounds and how they factor into which side of the dilemma you choose. Have your wounds made you more cautious or more daring? What if you were to go a different route? Think back to your earlier life dilemmas and consider what your life would look like if you had taken the other path. Do this as a way to help yourself see that the choice you made served a purpose. When you think about what life would be like had you decided on the other path, you begin to see the value in the decision you made because you know there's no going back. It is still good, however, to imagine what the other path would have looked like. At this point in your life, what would you say are some of the most pivotal dilemmas you've faced that led you to where you are now?

What if you could learn to use your past story to propel your dreams? What if your story could contribute to your professional success today? Is there a thread that links your story to either what you do or maybe what you want to do?

One of my favorite books on this subject is *The Millionaire Messenger* by Brendon Burchard. Brendon used his dramatic story to drive him to create a multimillion-dollar company. It all started with a near-death experience that led him to write a book, *Life's Golden Ticket*. After a near-death car accident, three questions came to him. Did I live? Did I love? Did I matter? This message led to him writing his book. This book led him to become the founder of his own company and to become one of the top business trainers and motivational speakers today. If you think your story empowers a business concept and you believe that you can utilize your story to build a following, I encourage you to do so.

Facing dilemmas and making choices is what determines our path in life. When we fall or go through a loss, we often discover in the process of healing that we needed the nudge. When we use our past wounds to help us make stronger decisions in the present and the future, we begin to see the true value behind our dilemmas. When we hit powerful enough dilemmas, the purpose behind them could be to get us to change our story. Since everyone has a story, why not write yours in a way that reflects what you want? I think dilemmas provide an opportunity to further define what it is that we want. They do this by often revealing what we *don't* want.

In its initial stages this book was going to be called *Turning Your Plan B Into Your Plan A*. Then, as the concept began to evolve, the title changed. Part of what inspired this change was reading the book *A Million Miles in a Thousand Years* by Donald Miller. I was mesmerized by the dilemma Donald faced after he wrote a best-selling memoir for which Hollywood came knocking. Movie producers wanted to make his book into a movie. At that time, Donald didn't feel that his life reflected how he wanted to be living in a deep enough way to be able to adapt his book into a movie. So he decided to change his story and live the life he wanted so that he had a strong perspective to write from. Donald's book goes into how he changed his story. I loved the concept of this so much that it inspired me to use my initial concept and mix it with the idea of changing your story. By using my twenty years of experience working with story construction, I could show my readers how using story tools could help them to change their story in order to live the life they wanted.

As I said earlier, dilemmas are where story begins. Your world is knocked off kilter. The journey of the story is to bring the life of the hero (your life) back into alignment. The hope is that you will be even stronger than you were before your starting dilemma. This is reflected in the stories you watch in films and on television as well as the real-life stories you live and experience around you. Powerful dilemmas lead to powerful change. If you are reading this book, most likely you've had moments when your world is turned upside down and life as you know it shifts. Your reality changes. You change. Your beliefs change. If you believed that "happily ever after" was the answer to your happiness, and then you experience it and discover that it is not, you go through a fundamental life change. You get married with the hopes of "happily ever after," but instead you end up divorced. You have your "happily every after" for only a moment instead of a lifetime. You are left with scars that make you link romantic love to pain instead of happiness. Your journey is to make stronger choices that lead you back to connecting romantic love to happiness.

Like many of you, my "happily ever after" moment fell short. Love visited me for only a short time. I felt betrayed and abandoned by love. For many years, I did not trust myself when it came to decisions of the heart. Part of my problem came down to the fact that I only really knew the external side of love. I had not really experienced the internal and spiritual side of love. I thought I recognized love but I later realized that my definition of love at that time in my life was based on a faulty philosophy. When I read this quote posted by Louise Hay, I realized that I only knew a certain side of what I thought was love: "Everyone says that love hurts, but that is not true. Loneliness hurts. Rejection hurts. Losing someone hurts. Envy hurts. Everyone gets these things confused with love. But in reality love is the only thing in this world that covers all the pain and makes someone feel wonderful again." I love the depth of this quote. It wakes us up to the reality of what we should feel when we are truly in love's presence. I hope to know this experience.

In the meantime, I try to value each experience that I have. There is a poem that inspired me during my healing from my divorce. It is titled *A Reason, a Season, or a Lifetime.* The author is anonymous. The first verse is: "People come into your life for a reason, a season, or a lifetime. When you figure out which one it is, you will know what to do for each person." These words helped me to view the dating experience in a different way. I do feel gratitude for the gift of each experience. I feel as if love has appeared, just not in a way that I could actively experience it. It's like waving candy in front of a child. You want to reach for it, but then the logical voice sees the obstacles involved. You feel the hurt and you lose your grasp. It is about doing the emotional work to stay connected to the belief that love will visit and love will stay when it is the right person. When love finds me again or when I find it, I want for both of us to be healthy, emotionally available, and open to the possibility.

A dilemma in your professional life is also a great starting point for your new story. You may know what it's like to put your life's work into one direction only to find one day that it is taken from you. This kind of loss can be detrimental; however, it comes down to how you choose to handle it. If you learn from the experience, you can move forward, even in a more authentic direction than you originally took. You can find greater rewards you may not have recognized had you not gone through your loss.

When I look at all of the entrepreneurs whose careers began with a story of loss or a story of change or a story of discontent, I see that there is something that links loss, failure, and rejection to a redefinition of goals, a new direction that is often better than the initial path, and oftentimes success on a major level. Why is that? When life takes a turn for the worse, it humbles you. It dilutes your ego and forces you to turn to your spirit. Your spirit is where your fulfillment lives. We need to learn how to balance the ego and the spirit and use what we learn from this process to change our story and change our lives for the better.

Dilemmas are your starting points for change. They wake you up. They frighten you. They humble you and leave you feeling vulnerable. They force you into a choice. The decision you make leads you down a new path. There will be bumps along the way. Learning that you can get over those bumps is part of your transformation. All of these feelings motivate you to move out of your pain and move back into pleasure. The journey of moving from pain back into pleasure can be a very long one; however, when you do the work, the gifts that appear along the way are countless. It is worth being present and moving through the pain in the quest of rejoining pleasure. After going through these emotions, your definition of what you view as pleasure changes. You can learn to steer away from pain if you heal and learn the lessons of what led to the loss. In essence, you can gain from the experience. When you move past pain, you grow stronger. When you grow stronger, you make better decisions. When you make better decisions, you gain back the belief in yourself that you may have lost. When you believe in yourself, anything is possible.

With the dilemmas you face, recognize the value in the lessons that come with them and that even though they might represent the end of one story, they also represent the start of a new story. All of your pain is there for a reason: to make you stronger and to provide growth. It is up to you to do the work and create the change you want to attract into your life. By moving through your dilemmas and learning how to create your new external goal from them, you gain clarity in what you don't want and in what you do want. With clarity comes action. As I've shown through my own story and the stories of others, using your past story can not only lead to a change in your new story, but can also lead to tremendous success on a physical, emotional, and spiritual level.

Exercise Four

Examine the dilemma that started your new story in Exercise One. How does the end goal of your new story link back to your starting dilemma? How will achieving your goal answer your starting dilemma?

Chapter Five

Putting Your Plan Into Action

Great acts are made up of small deeds.
— Lao Tzu

What is stopping you from being active in the pursuit of your goal? Being active after a fall is one of life's greatest challenges. In a story, the hero can be an anti-hero, a reactive hero, a passive hero, or an active hero. An active hero is the mark of a strong story. I want you to be an active hero in your life story. In order to be active, you have to view your obstacles in a new way. You have to change the script that accompanies your past. The wounds that result from your falls create obstacles. Often, a script accompanies your wounds and makes an imprint. You may think that if something happened before, there is a chance it could happen again. In order to bring something different into your life, you need to learn to change the script of your past and how you view your falls. Looking back at my "all is lost" moments I remember wondering if I had the inner strength to move through it all. What I have discovered is that my spirit has a limitless amount of strength. My ego is where the negative thoughts live. If I allow the voice of my spirit to be heard more clearly, then I can act from this place. Learning how to respond from your spirit will make a difference in your results. It all comes down to two words: take action.

Taking action is the key to your success. If you don't try, you will never know whether you could have accomplished your goal. The dilemma many of us face is that we shut down after we get knocked down and we stop trying. We lose momentum. We give up. We make excuses for why things can't happen. We find comfort in remaining inactive. We fear being rejected again or failing at another attempt. We find warmth in our cocoon. When we are not active, we feel like there is nothing to lose; however, by being inactive, there is even more to lose. The finite time that we have as human beings to leave an imprint or set a ripple will run out. We will end our lives regretting the many dreams that were never realized. By learning how to get over the obstacles that are preventing us from being active, we will see that by simply taking minor action on a daily basis toward our goals, we will be able to create the destiny we desire. By doing this, we will find our calling and our dreams will be realized. We will become the active hero in our own story.

As I mentioned earlier, on the road to becoming more active, you may hit the roadblocks of being reactive and passive. Are you just reacting to what comes your way? Does being passive make you feel safe? When you are active, you are acting with purpose and with an end goal in mind. For some, this is the only way they know how to be. For others, they connect with their fear instead. Does being active cause you anxiety? You think about when you were active in the past, how it led to a dead end, a mundane job, an unfulfilling relationship, etc. These thoughts all lead to a sense of failure. As I mentioned earlier, if you change the way you see your failures, you can begin to breathe easier and start the process of letting go of the negativity. It's all about conditioning your mind and spirit for greatness.

I remember hearing that behind every great leader there is often a string of failures. Hearing this made a pivotal change in my own life and my perception of failure. You can be great and fail in the process. Sumner Redstone of Viacom said that he learned more from his failures than his successes. I remember interviewing one very talented writer on my *Storywise* podcast. In my podcast I interview working writers in the industry so that they can share the stories behind their road to success. What I loved about this writer was that he admitted that he had been fired from just about every job he had ever had. The take away from this is that you can fail your way to the top. Where there is true talent, there is space for success. My yoga instructor, Jake Ferree, quoted something that I connected with: "You don't have to be great to start, but you to have to start to be great." Embrace this idea and the feeling of attaining your greatness. By focusing and defining a direction, you are taking a step. Putting your plan into action is everything when it comes to the success of your story.

In fiction, the character begins to take action after making a choice resulting from the dilemma and identifying a clear external goal that stems from that choice. The protagonist begins by taking action toward the goal. The stakes behind the action should be clear. These actions are what define his character and make him a hero.

In the movie *Crazy, Stupid, Love.*, written by Dan Fogelman, the character of Cal Weaver (Steve Carell) is shocked when his wife Emily (Julianne Moore) tells him that she wants a divorce. The dilemma that Cal faces is that he doesn't want one. To make things worse, his wife tells him that she slept with another man. We empathize with Cal from the very start of the film. His dilemma: Should he even try to win his wife back, or move on without her? Cal buries himself in his loss until ladies' man Jacob (Ryan Gosling) tells him that he's going to "show him how to get his manhood back" and make his wife regret the day that she put an end to their marriage. The actions that Cal takes to move himself closer to that goal is to change his wardrobe and to attempt Jacob's pick-up lines with women. It isn't until he realizes that honesty is his only game that he finally does land his first conquest. This helps Cal to regain his sense of manhood. Cal's son tells his dad that he needs to get his mom back. Cal then takes action toward this new goal, faces and overcomes his obstacles, and becomes the active hero in his own story.

Putting your plan into action is one of the most important steps you will take in your life and in your story. In order for real change to happen in your life, you have to create it. You have to move through your blocks, barriers, and excuses. You have to silence the negative chatter that says you can't do it. You have to learn to change those thoughts from the inside out. You have to really contemplate the question, "*What* do I want?" Then you have to consider your internal motivation: "*Why* do I want it?" Through visualization, you can imagine yourself at the other end of the achievement.

Learning how to be an active hero in your life story, and taking actions toward the new goal you've chosen, will lead you to creating the type of story you want your life to reflect. The starting point for being active is setting an end goal. In earlier chapters I've discussed mining your past experiences, looking at the external part of your goal (what you want) and the internal part of your goal (why you want it) as a way of further defining your intention. Now it's time to think about the present and how applying lessons from your past goals can inform your present and future goals. When you approach your daily life with clear intentions that lead you toward a goal, you are being active. Learning how to do this consistently in your own life is part of a healthy spiritual practice. How intentional and active are you in the pursuit of your goals?

One way to be more active is by defining your end goal through your life summary lines and story arcs. These are your roadmaps. In order to get to where you are going, you need to identify a destination so that you can take action toward it.

Start being active by reviewing your life summary lines and story arcs that you were introduced to in Chapter One and asked to write in the exercise at the end of Chapter Three. (See page 45.) Or, if you didn't do the exercise, you can write new ones knowing that these summary lines and story arcs will represent the first step toward changing your life by changing your story. Does your life summary line mean that you are limited to going in one direction? No. Sometimes your plans change when you are on the path to one destination or your motivation behind what you want changes. This simply means that through the act of defining an initial plan, you may find an even better plan that resonates more with you. As you begin moving in one direction, you may learn something along the way that drives you in a new direction.

Let's revisit the formula for your summary line:

— Set-up of "who" (present the protagonist and their strengths/ weaknesses)
— Dilemma
— Action
— Goal

A summary line is where I like writers to begin when they are about to start a new script or novel. A summary line is a tool to help you define your direction. In fiction writing, if your summary line doesn't work, then chances are when you go to the page, your story will not work. So why waste time thinking that you'll figure it out in the process of writing your story, and then get frustrated when you can't? Instead, why not just start with identifying what it is your central character (you!) wants. After that, it's just about mapping your way to the end goal through the journey of the story.

The same is true with the summary line for your life. Why just go into your life without taking the time to understand your intention behind each action you take? When you act without a plan, you are essentially responding to what life brings you. There can be beauty in just going along with what life brings you; however, this experience can also make you feel like you're in limbo, just reacting to what life brings your way instead of taking an active lead in the direction you want to go. Identify what you want first, and why you want it. Then design a plan and put it into action. How will you get from point A to point B? You are the author of your life.

I'd like to share with you a summary line that reflects a moment in my past that led me to the present moment. "After an ambitious yet overworked and disillusioned studio executive loses her job, she redefines her direction by opening her own company and helping others to realize their dreams while simultaneously realizing her own." My starting dilemma was created from the loss of my job. There were two sides to this dilemma. I could continue on my executive path and look for executive positions in an effort to move toward my initial goal of running a studio. Or I could create my own path by starting my own business and creating something that is in alignment with my internal goals and value system. My external goal of starting my own company stemmed from this dilemma. So by writing this summary line, I put a plan in place. By identifying my destination, I became an active hero.

Next, I want you to revisit the story arc you wrote in Chapter Three or consider writing a new one. Your story arc will allow you to go into more detail, helping you decide on your plan to get you where you want to go. Remember, the formula for your story arc is:

1. Starting dilemma
2. External goal stemming from dilemma
3. Thematic question
4. Actions taken
5. Obstacles hit leading up to your "all is lost" moment
6. External and/or internal stakes
7. Attainment of your goal

After losing my job as a studio executive, I took so many actions to create a new story. My story arc started with the loss of my job and facing the dilemma of what to do next. The first action I took was to heal the wound by going to Italy and to the Esalen Institute in Big Sur. I processed the pain. I wept. I let myself feel an array of emotions. I began the process of letting go. I took inventory of my life in that moment. I envisioned what I wanted my life to look like after this perceived fall. I let myself play. I got back in touch with why I loved what I did in the first place. I imagined the perfect job that involved doing only the things I loved the most about my old job. I defined an external goal. I would start my own company that focused on helping others with their individual visions while I would re-define my own. I thought of the thematic question I was going to explore with this new direction: Could I redefine my identity by creating a business that was all about doing what I loved to do? The thing I loved doing the most was developing story.

By identifying my expertise, I was able to find a niche in the market. I did the research. I designed a plan. I put my plan into action. I interviewed people who were where I wanted to be. I went to seminars. I worked with a website designer on my website. I read every book out there on business and marketing. I worked on defining my voice in a way that would separate me from the rest. I opened my business at a vulnerable time. I hit obstacles. I learned what does and doesn't work. I learned that I could get over obstacles. I recognized the external stakes if I failed to achieve my goal: I would have to find a job working for someone else again. I did not want to risk having my destiny in the hands of another. This fueled me even more. I saw success. My clients sold scripts and signed with representation. Things worked. The niche was being filled. Today I continue to see results in my clients and their careers. I breathe life into my creation every day. Now, what if I had decided not to go out on my own? I would have never known the beauty of this life experience or the fulfillment of achieving this success through my own vision.

Part of putting your plan into action involves thinking about the pain being caused by not moving forward. After my loss, I considered my identity. If I am not Jen Grisanti the TV executive, who am I? I am a daughter. I am a sister. I am a friend. I am a woman who still has big dreams. I am a woman who desires to fall in love. I am a spiritual being. I am a person with a limitless amount of love to give. I am more than a title. So are you. Titles limit us. One of the many things I love about writing my new story and putting my plan into action is the idea of being able to point all sides of my life in one new direction versus splitting the professional and the personal and having them live so independently, creating a rift within myself.

When we have two separate sides of ourselves, we are often in conflict. Our professional selves might have to do things that go against our spirit. In our personal lives, we are often trying to make up for what we are lacking in our professional lives. In order to make up for this or to try to find balance, we drink, we shop, we work out, we work harder, and anything else we can do to numb ourselves. We escape. Does this sound familiar in your life? If so, I want you to look at what the cost is of splintering off in two different directions. What if you could unite your two selves into one, so that your professional reflects your personal and your personal reflects your professional, and the conflict between the two lessens while the whole ignites? You can learn from both sides of your life. You can create divine peace between the two. You deserve to be in less conflict with yourself. You deserve to be feeding and fueling your possibility instead of dividing yourself in a way where neither side is ever fulfilled.

Let's start with your latest summary line and your external goal. What do you want? What does your perfect picture entail? I think this question stymies most of us. Yet it is so simple. I think we are socialized to believe that going after what we want is a selfish endeavor. Yet, really, how can we afford to not be doing what we really want or love? Why would we hold ourselves back from feeling true happiness every day when we wake up to do what we love to do? As many people have said, find what you love first, the money will come.

Now, I want you to think about your internal motivations connected to your new external goal. Why do you want what you want? What are your emotions underneath the desire? Could these same emotions be fulfilled with a different outcome? Do you think your internal motivations are in alignment with your external goal? When you visualize achieving your goal, what do you feel? What do you want to feel? Why are these emotions important to you? When you dig deep and go beneath what it is you want and why you want it, it will help you to clearly see what will motivate you into action.

Before embarking on my new path I had a clear look at my motivations behind my external goal. Professionally, I knew I wanted to work on my own and be my own boss. I wanted the feeling of independence and empowerment. I wanted to find value on the market for the seventeen years I had put into my career and all the knowledge I had accumulated up to that point. I wanted to add more meaning to my life and the lives of others through my new career. I wanted my new direction to reflect my ethics and life values. I wanted to make money because of the recognition that with money comes freedom. With freedom I could write the story that I wanted my life to reflect. Looking at my motivations helped me to see that moving in this direction — even though it was going to involve overcoming big obstacles — was worth it to me. I had already suffered a cost for some decisions I had made earlier in my life. I wanted to learn from that cost and grow into my new possibility. I wanted to change. This was the first step: looking at my reasons for wanting to achieve my goal.

With regard to change, where do you want to see change in your life? I talk about change in terms of personal and professional. On the personal side, there are many of us who want to make changes. Maybe we want to make changes in our finances, we want to change the way we choose who we date, we want to be happier, we want romantic love, or we want to make more friends and have a stronger sense of community... the list goes on and on.

On the idea of personal change, we may want to make changes that affect our physical appearance; for example, we'd like to gain or lose weight. Let's explore this. If you want to lose weight, think about the discomfort associated with keeping the weight on. Write down the emotions you feel resulting from carrying extra weight. Write down the things people have said that hurt you. Write down how food makes you feel. Then write down what you think you would feel by losing the weight. Write down how you think the change could make your life better. Write down the emotions you think you would feel if you lost the weight. If you want to gain weight, write down your answer to the same questions. Why do you want to gain? How do you think it will make you feel? What do you lose if you don't go after it? I believe that body image is something that affects all of us.

In my own life, weight used to be a bigger issue. I've learned to balance and accept. I touched on this earlier; however, now I'd like to go more into the action I took as a result of the dilemma. When I was younger, I was always thin and active. Then, I was in an accident at the age of 10. I put on weight as a result of the medication. My body changed. I remember the pain that came with this. Since people were used to seeing me one way, when they saw me another way, they made fun of me. Kids don't know any better. They say what they feel. So, by age 12, I began starving myself. I saw that when I was thin, I felt more loved. This started an eating disorder that lasted until I was 22 years old. I battled with bulimia and anorexia. I remember the rollercoaster of emotions that went along with this. When I was thin, even though I felt in control of my body, I really wasn't. At my lowest point I weighed 86 pounds. I had lost my breasts and stopped having my period. I recently read that part of the psychological trauma behind anorexia and bulimia is the fear of growing up. By starving yourself, you put your body back into a pre-adolescent state. This made sense to me. I had fear of moving away from home. I had fear of life changing. My body was the one thing I could control. So how did I stop? I weighed the pain versus the pleasure of what I was doing.

I remember living with three roommates in college; two of them had an eating disorder as well. One day I read about Jane Fonda and what bulimia had done to her. Then there was the sudden death of Karen Carpenter. These two moments had a pivotal effect on me. I thought to myself, is there anything good that is coming from this disorder? No matter how thin I was, I still felt insecure. So one day I just stopped starving myself, and then I stopped binging. I saw that the pain from staying like this was far greater than the pleasure I was receiving from it. I learned how to manage my weight through a healthy diet and exercise plan. This made me feel far better. I used the pain versus the pleasure to help me take action and make a change.

Today, health is a huge part of my life. I love eating healthy because of the way it makes me feel. I understand the balance between eating a healthy diet and working out. I take steps to learn about nutrition. I believe the food we eat is like medicine toward the aging process. I love changing and growing and being conscious of all of it and, above all, accepting my body for what it is and having gratitude for all the things it allows me to do. To come from an eating disorder and to move into this much healthier way of thinking took time and discipline. I did the work to make the change.

In my story, when I started my own company, I didn't know it would be the success that it is today. When I put my plan into action, I was jumping off one of the biggest cliffs of my life. I didn't have the financial backing if my plan didn't work. I didn't allow myself to think, "What if this doesn't work?" I had to believe that it would work. As crazy as it sounds, I knew from the beginning that I could be onto something big. I remember moving into a new place and thinking, I am going to build my company from the ground up. I am going to make my fortune while living in this place. I am going to put in the time that it will take. I am going to love the process. Drawing from my experience of becoming a high-level executive and seeing that it wasn't the ultimate destination I had envisioned for myself, I learned that the beauty is in the journey. I knew that what I had learned from some of the biggest and most celebrated storytellers in the business had market value that could change the lives of others and help them to achieve their dreams. By thinking about the pain of not going after my dream and, in essence, not being able to help others achieve theirs, I was able to see that there was only one direction for me to go.

When you desire change, you have to be willing and open to move through the discomfort of taking action and hitting hurdles in order to find comfort. What are you willing to do to change your story?

Are you willing to move out of your current reality and move into your future possibility? Do you feel that by putting your emotions into play you can use them to motivate you to write the story that better reflects what you dreamed about as a child? Can you see yourself changing? Do you see yourself going in a more authentic direction? In my own experience of personal transformation, I feel that I am becoming more conscious of moving from my ego to my spirit. It takes daily practice. When I am able to recognize that I am responding from my ego, I find that it takes great awareness to be able to shift back to spirit. When we are able to do this, growth occurs.

Think about your life. In which area of your life would you like to take action? It might be the personal or the professional, or it may be both. You can do it. Maybe you've achieved the professional results you wanted in your life and now it's time to focus on fulfilling the personal side of life. Maybe you already have your marriage, your kids, and your career, so now it's time to create a new story that expands your picture beyond what you initially imagined. It's all about using your pain of staying in your story as a way to help you move out of it. It's all about seeing the value in your dilemmas and knowing that instead of them holding you back, they can move you forward.

By understanding the internal and the external motivations behind what you want, you can better understand the true value of putting your plans into action. It also comes down to your motivation to move from pain into pleasure. Think about the external and internal stakes if you don't put your plan into action. Change the scripts from your past. Understand that your past does not equal your present. You can write a new story. You can be active in your pursuit of your goals. When you put your plans into action, you create your possibility. When you achieve your dreams, you are able to move into a higher place of consciousness and can use the lessons you learned along your path to help others to do the same. When you do this, you will find your calling and your purpose.

Exercise Five

What are the actions you will take that stem from the starting dilemma that you identified in your story and will lead you to the achievement of your goal?

CHAPTER SIX

Embracing Your Turning Points and Facing Your Obstacles

Be content with what you have; rejoice in the way things are. When you realize there is nothing lacking, the whole world belongs to you.

— *Lao Tzu*

I remember the moment that I began to embrace my turning point after the loss of my job. I was on my way home from Esalen, driving south along the California coastline. The ocean seemed to expand forever. I saw endless possibility. I loved the peace that washed over me. I recall embracing all of the lessons I had learned over my five-day stay. It evoked the feeling that I could take this fall and turn it into a gift. I could redefine my life and move in a more authentic direction. I knew that I had a ton of work ahead of me, especially if I was going to build my own company from scratch. Suddenly, I felt ready to do the work. I was refueled. For the first time in my life I felt that I could create a direction where no one could stop me from doing what I wanted to do.

When you learn how to embrace your turning points and face your obstacles, you recognize that you can turn a negative experience into a positive one and that you can create something new from a higher level of consciousness. Your life turning points are moments when suddenly you discover that the direction you were going in is no longer a strong direction for you to take. You may fall. The wind might get knocked out of you. Your life may feel as if it's going in reverse. Your sense of direction is thrown off balance. Sometimes these turning points are self-motivated. You are not happy with a certain outcome. You don't feel fulfilled. It's not what you thought it was going to be. You find yourself stuck or at a dead end. There is nowhere to grow. You recognize that in order to move forward, you need to make a change.

Sometimes your life turning point is out of your hands. Others make the decision for you, and you feel blindsided. You were on a path, moving toward what you thought you wanted. Then suddenly something changes; your world stops. The obstacle feels insurmountable. It could be something inside of you. Did you go down the wrong road? Did you stop valuing your path, or did the value in your path dwindle? Was the turning point your choice or someone else's?

With your turning points comes a state of transition. Your life is thrown out of alignment. Now, the journey for you in your new story is to learn to bring your life back into alignment. By doing this, you will become an active hero. In fiction, we start the story with the moment that triggers the journey on which our hero is about to embark. The goal is to bring his life back into order. The hero is going to face obstacles on the way to his goal. He is going to learn that through embracing his turning points and facing his obstacles, he will experience a strong sense of growth on the way to his goal. I want you to think about this when it comes to writing your new story. How do you view yourself when your story starts? How will you view yourself when it ends?

In the movie *The Sessions*, written by Ben Lewin, the lead character, Mark O'Brien (John Hawkes), who must use an iron lung due to polio, is asked to write a series of articles on sex and the disabled. While embarking on this journey, Mark decides that he wants to lose his virginity. With the help of his priest (William H. Macy) he contacts Cheryl (Helen Hunt), who is a professional sex surrogate. What follows is a heartfelt pursuit toward understanding what intimacy is on this level. It is a beautiful story. We feel for Mark with every obstacle he encounters. We think about intimacy in our own life. What was our first time like? What do we take for granted? We root for Mark to face his obstacles so that he can attain his goal of experiencing intimacy at a deeper level. The fact that the pursuit was clear from the start and something that we could all connect with made this movie even more special. It is a stunning exploration of a single life moment that can lead to so much more.

In my own life experience of facing my obstacles, turning points, and transition periods, I've found that there are four things you can do to turn a negative experience into a positive, life-affirming one. I want you to think about these points to help you through your transition and to guide you when you are writing your new story. These points are the ones that the hero often faces in their journey on the way to achieving their goal:

- Embrace the change
- Face your obstacles
- Believe
- Take action

Embrace the Change

By embracing the change, you are triggering the start of your new direction. I've learned that there is beauty in learning to embrace your turning points. There is so much to take in and process during your moments of change. You are raw. You are vulnerable. You are alive. You are sensitive. Just know that you will be all right. Find peace in knowing that you are exactly where you are supposed to be. Your turning points provide you with a gift; you just have to be open to receiving it. When a turning point first happens, you may experience a euphoric type of feeling. Maybe you worked for most of your life and the idea of not working is a fantasy, even if it's just for a moment. Maybe you were in a marriage that you knew was at a dead end but you wouldn't make the decision to end it on your own. You waited for something to happen that caused it to end. You feel euphoric for a moment when it does. You are free. After the highs you go through the lows of thinking, what is next? What if you can't think of a stronger direction to go in? What if all the time and effort you just put into this direction doesn't have meaning? What if you don't fall in love again? When you are in a state of transition, you are often very open. You are out of balance. When you are in this state, you have the flexibility to go in one new direction or in many. You move through a state of just being and embracing the present moment. You adjust to the transitional phase you are in.

When your alignment is thrown off balance, you need to recognize that you *will* get back to being steady. This is what the exercise of writing your story will help you to do. It will teach you how to respond to your turns and your obstacles in a new way. In the moment, being out of balance can have its rewards. You see things differently after being humbled. You notice kindness from others even more during this time. The kindness is always there; you just can't always see it. When you are raw, everything becomes clear. It's like every act of kindness is exaggerated and has more depth and meaning than it did before. That's because you feel weak. It's all right to feel weak and to ask for help. It's all right to need someone. It's all right to be in a state of limbo. During these times your truth often reveals itself even more. Your truth is your friend. It is your barometer. It will guide you back to a state of balance. Your truth is what will allow others to connect with you.

In the film *A Separation*, written by Asghar Farhadi, a married couple must face the dilemma and decide whether they should better their daughter's future by moving to another country or stay in Iran and look after a parent who has Alzheimer's disease. The story begins when Nader (Peyman Maadi) and his wife Simin (Leila Hatami) apply for a separation as a result of them wanting different things. The question becomes, will their daughter go to live with the mom or stay with the father? The first order of business after Simin moves out is for Nader to find someone to take care of his father. Simin makes a recommendation. A guy is hired. When he fails to show up on the first day, his wife, Razieh (Sareh Bayat) shows up instead. A few days in, an incident occurs between Nader and Razieh that could threaten both of their standings in the community. The goal is to bring the life that existed before all of this back into order. Many obstacles are encountered. One of the obstacles that Nader has to face is when his daughter asks him point blank if he lied about the incident with Razieh. I love the moral ramifications that are explored in this story. I love the strength of the obstacles, because in some circumstances there is no clear-cut answer to what is the right thing to do. This movie tells a very compelling story where we see the hero learn to face tremendous obstacles and embrace his turning point.

For me, embracing my turning point was an ongoing process. I remember the moment when it began, but I also remember realizing that acceptance would take continuous effort. There were so many lessons to learn on a professional and personal level. I did go through "crazy" moments. I made good choices, and I made bad choices. I learned. I grew. I knew this was all right. It was my time to just be without anyone's expectations about what my next steps should be. It was my time to flourish after the fall. I had to continue being open to doing the emotional work involved. One of the things that helped me move forward was taking inventory of why I made the choices I did and how I could learn from them instead of repeating the patterns that were no longer working for me.

Facing Your Obstacles

What if you could learn that your obstacles were leading you toward success instead of preventing it? Would this change your life? Facing your obstacles builds your confidence and, more often than not, moves you closer toward your destination. When I learned to move toward my obstacles instead of away from them, I was able to make changes in my life. By learning to face what I feared the most, I was able to dilute the fear and get results. Obstacles serve as stepping stones toward your goals. In fiction, they are a big part of what will make the story a success. You want to believe that your hero has the strength to face and get over her obstacles. In your story, you are the hero. You do have the strength to face obstacles. Obstacles are a significant part of the journey on your way to the goal because learning that you can get over them will be part of bringing your world back into balance.

When you experience obstacles in your story, you begin to see that even though it may start out as an external obstacle, there are internal ramifications. I would say that almost every external obstacle you face has an internal component. Both challenge you on many levels. They are put in your way to test your endurance and see if you have what it takes to reach the finish line. They deepen your life experience and show you that you are capable of so much more than you ever thought possible.

Let's look further into the internal side of your obstacles. In fiction, the internal obstacle is an obstacle that gets in the way of *why* your central character wants what they want. Moving through internal obstacles is what increases the strength of the hero to achieve the goal. In your story, identify the internal blocks that are getting in the way of your achieving your goal.

An internal obstacle in the way to many of our goals is happiness. The desire to feel happiness is what motivates most of us toward our goal in one way or another. Some of the obstacles I have placed in the way of my happiness include believing that when I accomplish something specific, I will feel happy. I think I did this more when I was younger. I believed in the fairy tale. I assumed that we would all get our "happily ever after." When mine didn't last, I experienced loss in a deeper way than I had ever experienced pain. I felt at times during my divorce that I had to relearn how to be happy. I had to learn to laugh again and rediscover my sense of humor. I threw myself into my career. I attached happiness to reaching certain pinnacles, titles, and accomplishments. What I learned was that these moments did not result in eternal happiness. They only brought me momentary happiness. Recognizing that certain accomplishments weren't the answer, I learned to let go of the expectation that I was attaching to happiness and just be in it. When we learn not to attach emotions to external outcomes, we set ourselves free.

I would recommend reading *The Happiness Advantage* by Shawn Achor, one of the leading experts in the field of positive psychology. Shawn essentially blows apart the idea that we are genetically predisposed to being happy. He shows through a series of principles that happiness can be learned. He writes, "Remember, happiness is not just a mood — it's a work ethic." Achor continues, "So how do the scientists define happiness? Essentially, as the experience of positive emotions — pleasure combined with deeper feelings of meaning and purpose. Happiness implies a positive mood in the present and a positive outlook for the future. Martin Seligman, the pioneer in positive psychology, has broken it down to three measurable components: pleasure, engagement, and meaning." Some of the activities he cited that impact our level of happiness include meditation, finding something to look forward to on a daily basis, committing conscious acts of kindness, infusing positivity into our surroundings, exercise, spending money on social experiences that will fulfill us (vs. material things), and giving positive feedback to those around us.

I love this book and its exploration of how we can learn to be happier. I think happiness is an internal obstacle that plagues all of our lives at one point or another. You know it is a state that you want to be in, but sometimes you forget the path to it because you get lost in your wounds, and you lose sight of (and appreciation for) all that you have. If you're lucky, you only experience short periods where you are not in a happy state. If you are not so lucky, it is more of a work in progress throughout your life. The good news according to this book is that if you do the work, you will succeed in finding happiness.

Resistance is definitely another internal obstacle worth exploring. What do you resist in your life? What stands in the way of you creating the story that you know you deserve? What obstacles do you use to create resistance to your goal? Steven Pressfield wrote a wonderful book on this subject called *Do The Work*. Steven is the author of another great book, *The War of Art*. Both books explore the word "resistance" and the things that artists do to get in the way of their art. Many of the obstacles he explores are internal obstacles dealing with negative self-talk and other behaviors that get in the way of our success. When you learn how to move through resistance and look at why you felt it in the first place, you can move into a stronger sense of awareness of how to move through resistance in the future.

Once I started my own company, I would say that my internal obstacles had to do with facing my fear of failure. I felt as if my ego had been deflated from the loss of my job. During the healing of this loss, I had gained the tools to move more into my spirit. I had to rebuild my belief from the inside. I had gained the confidence to be a TV executive, and now I had to gain the confidence to be an entrepreneur. I had to learn to believe that there was a strong market for the niche I was creating and that I could rebuild what I had lost. The difference was that this time it was all up to me. To help me move over the fear, I read books by authors including Seth Godin, Alan Weiss, Eckhart Tolle, Brendon Burchard, Tony Robbins, Wayne Dyer, Marianne Williamson, Dr. Sue Morter, Robert Cooper, and Jerry Weissman. Hearing their stories and how they were able to overcome their obstacles inspired me in the beginning.

I knew that by building my career in a more authentic direction, with my motivation going toward helping my clients write their best material without an agenda attached or connected to something else, that I really could learn the beauty of coming from my spirit. Because I was coming from my spirit, I knew that obstacles would feel more surmountable because I had learned to rely less on my ego and this would help me to overcome the obstacles.

Now, I've mentioned that my personal life is definitely an area that I want to work on in terms of changing my story. The obstacles faced after a betrayal and a divorce tend to run very deep. They can be forgiven, but the scars are not forgotten. Once trust is broken, it's a long road to learning to trust someone again. For me, when I hear things in other men's stories that remind me of my ex-husband, it frightens me and makes me move away from the possibility of a relationship with them. I am afraid that I will repeat a pattern, and if I do, that I will get the same outcome. Yet, I try to always remind myself that everyone has a different story and that I have to be open. I know that when I committed myself to my professional goal 150%, things happened for me in a major way. I was able to redefine myself and recreate a job that is filled with everything I love. Now, I know that if I take the same kind of care, discipline, and dedication in my personal life, I can face my fears and create the same kind of change in my personal story. It all comes down to learning to get over the internal obstacles that are preventing me from moving forward. So this is still a work in progress as I write this book. While I am encouraging you to change your story and change your life, I am hoping to do the same in my personal life.

Believe

Believing that your new direction can be more authentic than your initial direction is part of what will motivate you toward the external goal in your new story. Oftentimes, when you really think about it, the direction that you were going in may not have been in alignment with your spirit. Perhaps it was more in alignment with your ego. Maybe you were on a personal or professional path you thought you were supposed to be on or that you just ended up taking due to circumstances. You were seeking security and stability and the path you took seemed to be the answer. When we are younger, we believe that the answers are on the outside. As we get older, we see that they are all within. We just have to have the courage to go there. So, as a result of your turning points you have an opportunity to start a new chapter and embrace a new path. If you can draw from what you learned in the old path, you might discover that the new path can be more authentic and utilize your strengths and values in a way that the other situation didn't. When you take the time to process your turning points, you strengthen your spirit. By healing your spirit and strengthening it, you start to believe again. When you believe anything is possible, then it becomes so. In order to get to this point of my journey, I found that it was beneficial to go through all of the other phases first so that I was prepared to be in this phase of my transition.

Sometimes your turning points cause you to take a step backward before you can move forward. It is all right to move backward. Think about it: When you take a step backward, you feel the comfort of the "known" again. You have a really positive moment that makes you feel as if the negative has ended. Then you wake up the next day and something happens that awakens the wound all over again. It's all right. It means that there is more work to be done. It is a reminder that the wound is still open. It's all right to respond. It's all right to feel crazy. We all go through feeling crazy when we are trying to get better. You must realize that there is no shame in moving backward, especially if it is in an effort to move forward. Every hero experiences at least one major setback — that's an inherent part of a hero's journey.

Taking Action

The fourth thing I want you to think about as you are transitioning out of your turning point and facing your fears is taking action. By taking action, you begin to create a new path, a new reality, and new possibilities. You become the hero of your story. I think that many of us want to take action immediately because we want to stop the pain. We don't want to do the work; instead, we just want to arrive on our new path and begin moving in any given direction. If we take the time to do the emotional work before we take action, we are better equipped emotionally and spiritually to handle the change and move forward, often in a stronger direction than we were going before.

Now I'd like to jump back into the stories shared by the respondents of my questionnaire and the actions they took after hitting some pivotal life turning points.

After being born into a dilemma resulting from her parent's extra-marital affair, Rosemary went on to cheat on her husband. This is what she writes about having her own affair: "Thirty years later, I was an officer's wife, married to a man who cheated on me over a dozen times. We had three children. I was unhappy but determined to do right by my family and God. I stayed with him for ten years. But then I had my own affair and my own love child. I left my husband. I was excommunicated from my church, my mother stopped talking to me, my brother, who is a pastor, did everything he could to get me back on 'the right track.' My brother believed my family was cursed because of what my parents did thirty years before. With no parents, no siblings, no God, and no support from anyone, I imagine I got a taste of what my mother went through. I struggled with guilt, suicide, and fear of damnation." The actions that she took after this turning point were studying Neale Donald Walsch's *Conversations With God* and writing in her journal daily.

Stephen's turning point happened when he experienced eye trauma that led to serious retinal detachments, resulting in three months of remaining stationary, and the risk of blindness. Stephen describes what happened as a result of his turning point: "As a result, I became grateful for the ability to have sight. I also was amazed by the richness of the internal landscape, impressed by how quickly the other senses make themselves more known when one sense is lost. I experienced a non-judgmental state where communication came from the heart and went unmeasured by visual cues of how one is being received during a conversation."

Diane's story involves three turning points: "I'd be happy to share some grist for the mill — end of a marriage, death of a parent, pregnant teen-age daughter; a midlife trifecta, all in the last two years. I'm a writer; I write my way through everything, and this is no exception, but sometime after we lost my father last fall, my journals began to change. Inspired by Tolstoy and fueled by Joseph Campbell, I started looking at my life as if it were a story. The themes, the thresholds, the metaphors; it was all right there. That was a game-changer for me. I may not know how to cure pancreatic cancer, but I damn sure know how to handle a plot device. I started writing my own hero's journey, ripe with obstacles and aid and dragons and grails. When I say it's a mighty experience, I suspect you know what I mean. Your title echoes Leo Tolstoy's sentiment, 'If you want to work on your art, work on your life.' Working on my life as if it were my art is both. Two birds, one stone; the Virgo in me loves that efficiency. The shrink in me loves the personal growth, and the writer loves a fully realized character arc. You can change your story. You can change your life. In each, honesty is the key to authenticity."

The action that I took after losing my job (and after doing the emotional work to process the loss) was to start my own business. This was a huge step for me. This was going down a whole new path. When I officially started my business, it was seven months after I had left my previous job. So it was in those seven months that I went through all of the steps I mentioned that led to me being ready to take action again. In starting my own business from scratch, I had to educate myself in an entirely new direction. I had to learn the business side behind it all. Although I knew that the core of my business would involve giving notes on story, which was everything I had learned and loved in my old career, I had to understand what this new direction would involve on all levels. Learning how to run a business has been fascinating. I have to admit, I thought that the administrative parts would bore me and take me away from the creative side. I have discovered, however, that knowing and understanding everything that is going on in my business is empowering. This makes me look back at the turning point that resulted in this new direction with nothing but complete gratitude.

Now it's time to think about your story. In fiction and in life, turning points and obstacles are there for a reason. They serve a tremendous purpose. They cause us to move from one world into another. They are there to help us to grow and to move us in a stronger direction. By learning to be active after your turning point and as you face your obstacles, you are creating a new possibility. In doing this, you become the active hero in your own story.

Exercise Six

What are the two biggest external obstacles that you see yourself facing on the way to achieving the goal in your new story? What are the two biggest internal obstacles?

CHAPTER SEVEN

Identifying Themes in Your Life

We must be willing to get rid of the life we've planned, so as to have the life that is waiting for us. The old skin has to shed before the new one can come.

— *Joseph Campbell*

I often think of the themes that run through my life. Sometimes I am conscious of them when they appear. Other times I need them to revisit me many times before I can understand the meaning behind their presence. When I can feel the reopening of a past wound, I know that I still have a lesson to learn. There is still growth that needs to happen. Themes are invisible threads that weave together and add meaning to the outcome. I would say that resilience is a theme in my life. I know what it is to fall. I know what it is to get back up. I recognize that my fall was put in my path to make me stronger and to test my commitment to my direction both personally and professionally. Other personal themes that run through my life are my desire to give and feel unconditional love and my hope to trust again after experiencing betrayal. I find that I have a pattern that seems to repeat itself when it comes to love. I feel the message. I hear it. I am in the midst of moving with it instead of against it. I know that I need to change the negative inner chatter from the past that goes on in my mind in order to find the kind of success in my personal life that I have found in my professional life. I know I can do this. You can also bring change into your life by better understanding and identifying your recurring themes. Your themes are invisible guides that move you toward a higher place if only you will hear their voice and let them lead.

Themes are often something you are not aware of until they show up many times. Your themes are speaking to you. Can you hear them? Your themes are like a gentle reminder telling you that your philosophy has flaws. This is what could be holding you back from doing something greater.

In fiction, themes can be explored in so many different ways. A theme can be used in a story arc to create a thematic debate. By this I mean, in a well-told story there is often a thematic question explored by the writer that is answered by the end of the story through the experiences of the central character. They often move from one side of the spectrum to the other through hitting obstacles, being humbled, and discovering that they can change for the better.

In your story, the same thing may be happening. You might have a belief system that you cling onto, and through your life experiences the universe delivers messages that may allow you to loosen your grip on one belief as you begin to see that it is no longer serving you. Then, with openness, you embrace a new belief because you feel it may serve you better. If you are conscious or become more conscious of your recurring themes, you will recognize what they are and how you can utilize them to get to where you want to go in your life. Once you become more conscious of your themes, you can learn to shed belief systems that are holding you back and identify new ones that will move you forward. In this chapter, I want you to consider some of the themes I will explore by way of my own story and the stories of others. If you see yourself having the same theme, think about how you can replace it or learn how to master it. The question that I want you to explore is this: Can you identify a theme that is preventing you from moving forward and change it?

There are three things to think about in terms of themes in your life:

- Awareness
- Identifying whether your themes are moving you forward or holding you back
- Conscious endeavor

Awareness

In fiction, theme is a device used to tie together all the story lines and bring a greater awareness of what the writer is trying to say. When done well, it unites the overall feeling we get from watching the story. It deepens what the storyteller is trying to say and connects it all under an umbrella. When it is well integrated, the themes explored in any secondary story lines will elevate what is being explored in the central story. We are let into the writer's vision by how he connects his story lines. Theme helps us look at the belief systems of the characters. In doing so, we automatically attach our own belief system to how we react to the story. In any story, the writer debates a thematic question throughout. Sometimes it comes up in such an unexpected way, and when we identify it there is an emotional response to whether we agree or disagree with the writer's position in the debate.

With a debate comes awareness. When you are faced with a powerful dilemma and you make a choice, the themes that emerge from that choice are often what you are debating on a conscious or subconscious level. Did you make the right choice? Is it going to take you where you want to go, or is it going to lead you to a dead end? In the midst of the journey, will you awaken to what you need and see that more work may need to be done on an internal level in pursuit of your external rewards? Are you traveling down the right road? Is your philosophy enhancing your travel or getting in the way of it? When you ponder your own thematic questions with awareness, you increase your chances of making smarter choices in the future.

Most of us don't really even recognize the themes that come up in our lives until the universe has tried to repeat the message many times and in many ways. It might help you to think in terms of your own life: What are some of your recurring issues? What is a thematic question you are pondering right now in your life? For example, when it comes to relationships, what are some of your issues? What are things that come up in your experience? What is holding you back from having a positive relationship and finding true love? For me, as I mentioned earlier, I would say that trust is an issue due to my past experience with betrayal. Trust is a recurring theme in my life. A thematic question I am exploring is will I be able to open myself up and make the space for true romantic love in my life again? This stems from past wounds. As a child, like many of us, I trusted everyone. Then, after a number of situations taught me not to be as open, I began to see that trust is an issue I've never quite mastered. By recognizing this ongoing theme in my life, I can do the emotional work necessary to be more open to the idea of trust in my future relationships and separate it from my past. I want to move past my internal and external blocks that are contributing to this. I want to find an answer to my thematic question.

During a stay at the Wellness Immersion Retreat in Tulum, Mexico, I wrote a few chapters for this book. I shared with the other participants of the retreat that I was writing this book and that I was going to use some of the stories that resonated as a way to show the universal themes that we all experience. At the time, there were many themes that resonated with me. I think it is worth taking the time to explore the themes that surfaced during that week. Going into the experience, the theme was spirituality as it is connected to healing. Actions that supported this theme included our daily practice of yoga, writing, and painting. In addition to that, many themes surfaced during our group discussions. When you are at a retreat meeting new people, you find that you immediately connect to others because you are all seeking something to fulfill you on a deeper level. This quest bonds you. It also provides a reason to look at your story and extract from it the universal emotions and experiences that you share with the group. Lots of emotions surface during the exercises in this kind of experience. Emotional awareness becomes more prevalent. When we are conscious of what we're feeling and why we are feeling it, rather than numbing ourselves to emotional pain, we stand a much stronger chance of moving toward wellness and achieving our life's destiny.

At the beginning of the retreat, we often discussed the theme of self-doubt associated with our craft. Self-doubt is an internal obstacle that can clearly get in the way of our external endeavors. Self-doubt is something that is usually birthed from a childhood experience and/or wound. I think most artists have levels of self-doubt in their creative expression. I would actually say that most of us, if not all, have a wave of self-doubt that flows through our being from time to time. Rather than suppressing it, trying to fix it, or getting rid of it, I actually think it is a theme that could motivate us to produce our best work.

Similar to fear, self-doubt can be utilized as a driving force to your success. It is worth doing the emotional work to understand the past wound that is behind your self-doubt. By connecting with the core of what started the pain, you are able to forgive yourself for attaching to this and forgive the person involved in contributing to your inner conflict. Take action and think about a thematic question that explores self-doubt and why it holds you back in certain areas of your life. By identifying a theme in your life and seeing the obstacles it creates, you will be able to eliminate it.

Who were the people in your past that made you doubt yourself? Was this a lifetime experience of being with a person who couldn't help you see your own worth? Were you ever made to feel unlovable? Or did you begin to second-guess yourself as a result of a relationship that didn't work out? Is this something you can control? By exploring questions like these, you can learn to befriend the self-doubt you may feel and understand that it is just a temporary visitor. When it is there, you can utilize it to drive you further into your craft. There could be something to gain from it if you learn to change your perspective on it.

At the Tulum retreat, another theme that surfaced for me was resistance. For example, some of the yoga classes required that everyone work with a partner. Because of that, I found myself initially resisting this experience. I didn't want to have to work with someone else in what I viewed as a solitary practice. It was good for me to notice this in myself. At first the thought of adding a partner element to my practice made me uncomfortable; then it led me to push past my boundaries of physical contact, space, intimacy with a new friend, etc. It was an opportunity to move past some of the intimacy issues that have built up from my past wounds. After my divorce I became intensely independent. While learning to trust myself, I forgot the beauty and value in trusting others. Like anything, it took practice to learn how to be a partner again. As the week went on I began to look forward to the experience. I began to see the value of putting the energy toward making my yoga partner feel good in the process and I began to find more joy in what I was feeling inside. It gave me confidence. It made me realize that I could take what I learned from this partner experience and bring it back to my own life and apply it when necessary. By recognizing one of my themes, I was able to understand it more clearly and move past it.

Learning to be a partner again is a journey, just as relearning to be independent after breaking up with a partner is a journey. It definitely involves facing trust issues due to past emotional wounds. After experiencing the loss of trust in a partnership, you have to do the work to rebuild it. Actually, what you are rebuilding is self-trust in your ability to make good choices. When you go through a break up, you eventually learn to be independent again. You feel as if you are alone. Yet, if the relationship wasn't working, you were probably alone to begin with, you just couldn't see it. You need to recognize that you are all right and you will heal. After doing the emotional work, you will learn to be completely independent again. Self-reliance becomes a habit. You begin to feel that you are fine on your own and you don't need anyone because you've learned the value of making yourself happy. Suddenly the theme of wanting someone versus needing someone surfaces. You may feel that it's healthier to "want" versus "need." When you enter into a new relationship, that feeling of suddenly needing the other person might be powerfully felt. At this stage in my life I know that I want a romantic relationship, but I don't need it. At times I think that my pride and ego tell me I don't need a relationship because "wanting" is healthier than "needing." This awareness has led me to conclude that it is all right to want someone. And it is also all right to need someone.

Another theme that surfaced at the retreat involved the idea of wanting to have a child. Jade, one of our retreat leaders, discussed her journey with wanting to have a child. She said she examined her reasons for wanting a child; she had the desire to nurture, to teach, and to help a child realize their potential in order for them to contribute something great to the world. She realized that she was already doing this in her life's calling and that perhaps she didn't need to have a child to have this experience. I went through the same type of experience in my own life, so I identified with Jade's journey in a very deep way. I always thought that having a child was a definite part of my destiny. My reasons for wanting a child were similar to Jade's. I also felt that it was what I was supposed to do. It represented my "happily ever after." I thought having a baby would make my life more complete. As the years went on, coming to grips with the idea that motherhood was soon to be no longer in the cards for me biologically was a huge turning point. Learning to move into the acceptance of this was a process. I actually found freedom once I moved through the pain of letting it go. So hearing Jade put it this way helped me to connect with this theme in my own life.

There was another woman in the group who also identified with accepting that having a baby biologically might no longer be a part of her path. She told us that she had just had this conversation with a friend in Sweden who was soon turning 41. This demonstrated to me that there are millions of women and men going through the process of letting go of a life experience they thought was supposed to be a part of their path. Also, it showed me that they are finding other ways to fill that desire. By understanding the internal motivations behind why we want a child, we can better understand if our internal motivations can be satisfied in other ways and through other experiences.

Identifying Whether Your Themes Are Moving You Forward or Holding You Back

Countless themes emerged during the retreat in Tulum. Some themes were clearly holding people back in their lives while other themes were clear motivators moving people forward. While going through the stories of others and hearing about their themes, I want you to think about your themes. Can you identify the ones that are holding you back from being the active hero in your own story? If you can, try exploring a question that will help you to determine whether you want to eliminate the theme because it is preventing your growth or whether you want to embrace the theme because it is helping light your path.

One theme I noticed repeating itself in many of the stories shared by this group had to do with attaching so much to a romantic connection that our own expectations prevented the success of the outcome. This particularly came up in the writings of one woman. She was on a continuous quest for more romance in her life. She hoped that it would happen during her constant travels around the world. I am sure that every person in the room identified with this quest. You may know this quest too. You get swept up in the fantasy. When you travel, there is a sense of freedom. With this freedom comes openness. When you are open, magic is more likely to happen. You want to believe that true love is out there, and what better way to find it than when you are traveling. This quest might lead to different outcomes, but the idea is very universal. You may raise the bar so high by way of your expectations and connect so much to the outcome that the experience is almost never fully realized because of how you move toward it. If your quest is so focused on one outcome, you can miss experiencing the beauty of other things that may appear instead. By learning how to adjust your expectations, you can have a successful outcome.

For me, attaching the fairy tale and the feeling of "happily ever after" to my marriage is something that blocked me from fully experiencing all levels of what a marriage is. I had been conditioned through fairy tales and my romantic view of stories to believe that when you fell in love, certain things were supposed to come with this experience. You were supposed to feel a certain level of completeness as a result of the experience. After going through it, I realized that the feeling of completeness could only come from the inside, not from an outside person or situation. With the person we choose to connect with, we often see a reflection of ourselves. Sometimes, the reflection makes us see that there's more work that needs to be done internally in order to have a rewarding outcome externally. A lot of work went into coming to this realization.

For the young woman who shared her stories of finding romance abroad, my hope is that she understands that the external experience of meeting a romantic interest isn't always going to quench the internal desire she attaches to it. She is such a beautiful and happy person that I know what she is seeking will come her way when the time is right. In her story, I think the theme of attaching expectations to a specific outcome in her vision of romantic love is holding her back instead of moving her forward. I can identify with this hurdle.

A theme that surfaced in the personal story of another person at the retreat had to do with starting over. This woman had lived in five countries in the last ten years and mentioned everything that went into starting over in each place. This brought to mind the idea of new beginnings. I tried to imagine what it was like for this woman to begin again over and over. The idea of having to find a new circle of friends and of creating community with each move seems daunting. Yet, the idea of having a new opportunity to figure out who you are within the context of each place and each situation fascinated me. I connected with the desire behind it. I applauded her courage and her conviction. I found her ability to interpret the world to be very strong on the page. What this said to me was that the life experience of starting over really contributed and added great value to her voice. I think in some ways her theme is allowing her to move forward, but in other ways it is holding her back.

How we view the obstacles in our lives is a recurring theme for most of us. Do we view them as easy to get over? Do we give up once the obstacle becomes too much or the hurdle seems too high? When we fail to take action, we are often weighed down by things like too many choices, not enough time, financial obligations, family obligations, etc. These things just get in the way of our ability to take a risk and put a plan into action. I know that this is a very common dilemma with most people who want to write. They can't figure out how to make the time due to so many other extenuating circumstances.

I went through the same dilemma with writing each of my books. My business was growing by the day. I was in over my head with work and obligations, both personal and professional. How I learned to overcome this obstacle was to figure out a time when I could write that didn't interfere with all of my other responsibilities. For me, the solution was to get up as early as 4:00 a.m. so that I could get the work done before my other responsibilities came into play. This involved me going to bed on most nights as early as 9:30 p.m., but it was worth it. I identified how I felt about the obstacle of there not being enough time and I learned how to move through it.

Where there's a will, there's a way; you just have to be disciplined and have an end goal in mind that you're working toward. When you learn to see your themes as gentle reminders that could enhance your journey and allow you to see things more clearly, you grow on your path.

By taking the common theme of "lack of time" and figuring out a way to make the time and get it all done, you will be able to move forward.

Another story that resonated thematically involved life after a car accident. It came from a tremendously successful, very beautiful businesswoman at the retreat. There's a shift in how you see yourself in the world because of the physical and emotional trauma suffered as a result of illness or an accident. Apparently she was even more beautiful before the accident, so letting go of beauty in the way that she knew it was a journey for her. She had to go through countless reconstruction surgeries to get her face to a point of resembling how it looked before the accident. I imagine that there are all kinds of emotions that you go through with this type of life experience. I am sure that you ask yourself, "Why me?" This is natural.

When I heard this woman's story and thought about it in conjunction with all of the entrepreneurs who have had a tragedy guide them in a new, even more successful direction, it made me see the link. When we hit rock bottom and there's nowhere to go but up, we tap into a spirit and an inner strength that we probably didn't even know we had inside. When the way we see ourselves shifts as a result of something on the outside, there is so much internal work that needs to be done in order to find peace within ourselves, let go of the past, and find calmness in living in the present moment.

I found this woman's beauty to be even deeper in the present because of the emotional work she had done to move past this turning point. For her, I think the theme of how she views beauty held her back for a while. However, through doing the emotional work she's done and accepting that her beauty is not only reflected on the outside but something that comes from within, she is able to use this theme and her awareness of it to move her forward.

Another woman at the retreat shared a journal entry that touched my heart and the hearts of everyone in the room. Her theme involved an internal struggle with going down one path and succeeding in it, but at a cost to her personal life. This is a common theme that many of us experience in life. We make a choice that brings material wealth and allows us to provide for our families, but on the other hand, doesn't fill our spirit due to a lack of emotional connection with a loved one.

This woman went in pursuit of providing for her son, but in the process didn't have the time she felt she needed to actually be with him. She connected this to the outcome of her son using drugs and not being as productive as she had hoped he would be. Like many parents, she felt that if she could provide a comfortable living and a strong education that everything would fall into place. I could tell that she attached some shame to the fact that her pursuit of her career lessened her time with her son. This is a universal dilemma that many parents face.

From hearing my own parents talk, as well as all of my friends who are parents, I've learned that every parent feels, at one time or another, as if they are not doing enough; they could do better, they could be there more, they may have done something to cause a permanent scar, etc. This is all part of the process of being a parent. Seeing how it made this woman feel and the emotions that came out as a result of her sharing her experience tugged at my heart. For any parent, a common theme is balancing the roles they play and wondering if they can really be good at all of them. I believe if she can learn to let go of this belief that is holding her back, she can create the story she wants her life to reflect. As she read her journal entry, my heart connected because I was hearing the voice of the writer emerge with her truth.

In our journal readings and group discussions, the theme of desiring romantic love came up in several ways. Stories of lost loves and broken relationships emerged. Yet there was a sense of peace with regard to many of the past situations. I found there to be more anxiety expressed about the romantic love yet to come. Will it happen again? Will there be a second, or in some cases a third or fourth, chance at love? When will we fall in love again? Will we learn from our past relationships in a strong enough way to change the choices we make in the future? I like to believe that we all grow from our past relationships.

If we take the time to heal before jumping into another relationship, I think we increase our chances of success.

If you think about what you want internally from the external experience of love, you can find other ways to fill the desire in the meantime. That way, you can feel complete while waiting for the piece of the puzzle that will enhance your sense of completeness. You can calm the quest. Your themes about love may often hold you back instead of allowing you to move forward. However, by being aware of them and recognizing that you can use them to move forward, you can be more active in a positive outcome.

Conscious Endeavor

Another theme we explored was finding purpose. How do you know what your life's purpose is? Will you figure out what your calling is? A stronger question to ask yourself is, are you in pursuit of finding your calling? I've learned in my own life that in order to accomplish anything, you have to put in the work. You have to know what you want and go after it with everything you've got inside you. If you think about your path and the themes that arise from your pursuit of certain goals, both personal and professional, the answers are there. You just need to be open enough to trust in them and follow where they lead you.

Most professional writers need solitude and focus in order to do their best work. We need the same when writing our own life stories. I want to encourage you to discover retreats like the ones I've mentioned. Being in a safe place to explore activities like yoga, meditation, writing, and art, you will add clarity to your thought process. When you see yourself reflected in the stories of others, it enhances your vision of self. When you are in search of an answer, you often find it. Finding your purpose is a personal journey. To feel that you are living your life's purpose or calling is an ongoing search for millions of us. Yet the beauty of it is that we want to feel it. When you have the desire to know, you can find what you're seeking.

In your story, think about themes that consistently come up in your life. What are you hoping to feel with a certain outcome? What belief system do you cling to that may be stopping you from fully being in the present moment versus attaching your expectations to what the moment should be? Have you gotten comfortable with one way of thinking that you close yourself off to new ways? When you think about writing your story, think about using the method of moving from one emotion to another.

In your personal story, recognize the value in identifying your recurring themes. Recognizing themes when they appear can deepen your life experience. They shed light on things you may not have been aware of. Or they can be a debate that you are exploring in both sides of your life. You could find an answer to your thematic question that changes how you view things. The answer could move you from one perspective that is holding you back to an opposite perspective that could lead you toward your destiny. Themes are a gift that, when received with awareness, can open you up to limitless possibilities.

Exercise Seven

Identity the main theme you plan to explore in your new story and the thematic question that will come from it?

CHAPTER EIGHT

"All Is Lost" Moments

How Hitting Rock Bottom Can Lead You To Your Goal

It is by going down into the abyss that we recover the treasures of life. Where you stumble, there lies your treasure.

— Joseph Campbell

Your "all is lost" moment may feel like the end of your story, but is in reality the start of your final phase of reaching your goal. My "all is lost" moment came when, after being told that my job contract wasn't being renewed, I was asked to return to work for three weeks before my last day. Those were the longest three weeks of my life. I knew, and everyone else knew, that my climb toward running a studio was over. I didn't think that I would be able to go through with it, but the miraculous thing was that I needed to go to that "all is lost" feeling in order to finally see what I had to do. I learned what it was to hold my head up high and to face my fears. My "all is lost" moment led me to my life's purpose. Your "all is lost" moment can trigger the same for you.

In fiction, an "all is lost" moment is when the central character is as far away as possible from achieving their goal. As a result of hitting rock bottom, they have an epiphany of what they need to do to finally achieve the goal. There is a gift in hitting rock bottom. It's all about being open to receiving the message when you get there. You can rest assured that there will be a message. The question is, will you be open to hearing it? When we lose everything, we truly begin to see what our spirit is made of.

In the movie *Frost/Nixon*, written by Peter Morgan, there is a strong "all is lost" moment. The goal for the character of David Frost (Michael Sheen) is to get an interview with Richard Nixon (Frank Langella). His producer lets him know that if he gets the interview, the people will want a confession in order for it to be successful. Frost gets the interview. He hits many obstacles on his way to the goal. The "all is lost" moment is when Day 1 and Day 2 of the interview with Nixon are a disaster. Nixon continues to take control of the interview and ramble. David attempts to get more financing and is unable to do so. As this interview process is failing, Frost finds out that he has lost his job in Australia. He has one day left to get the confession or his interview will be a bomb. It is at this rock bottom moment that he gets a drunken call from Nixon that leads Frost to a victory and the achievement of his goal.

Think about your past "all is lost" moments. What did they look like? What did you do in order to move past them? Specifically, what actions did you take? Through hitting the bottom, did you find that you were able to use the fuel to go further than you ever thought possible? If not, I am going to show you how to do this.

Here are the five actions I want you to take after hitting rock bottom:

- Reassess
- Research
- Evaluate your internal motivations
- Define your goal
- Take action

Reassess

Think about one of your "all is lost" moments. What led you to it? What was the external goal that you were pursuing? Was your goal clear? What actions did you take in pursuit of your goal? Where did it go wrong? What do you think contributed to it going wrong? How can you learn from it? What message did you hear when you first hit rock bottom? Did you point the finger at someone else? Or did you look inside and think about what you may have done to contribute to the outcome? When we reassess, we become more conscious of how our actions may have contributed to the outcome.

While reassessing, it's important to look at the truth behind the outcome that was manifested, and your part in that truth. When you do this, you give your truth a greater chance of coming forward and shedding light that can help you avoid doing the same thing again in the future. Your truth often waits in the shadows until you are ready to bring it into the light. Sometimes you have to feel safe in order to live a life where your truth guides you; until the point you are ready to face it, you may be traveling in the darkness. Oftentimes, when the worst happens, a part of you wakes up and sees that there could be something better. Know that by being active you can move from the darkness into the light.

During your reassessment phase, think about the series of events and choices that led up to the outcome. Then look at your own involvement in what transpired. Your involvement is often the most important component in understanding why the outcome happened. You can only control your actions, so it is critical to look at them with an honest and fearless eye. What could you have done better? What will you do better the next time? I believe that we can all do better in all aspects. If we don't think that we have a chance to do better, then we don't have the desire to grow. Doing better is something I think about on a daily basis. How can I do better today than I did yesterday? There is no shame in this. It sets forth a positive intention and it is a way to stay active in your destiny.

In my own reassessment phase, after my career came to an end, I had to ask myself all the same questions I am asking you. I think my initial reaction was to point the finger outward. My ego did not want to accept that I had anything to do with the loss of what I considered at the time to be my dream job. I reacted out of fear because, in the moment, I felt as if my destiny was being taken from me and I didn't know how to respond to this kind of change. What I didn't realize then, but I do now, is that this loss would actually be to my benefit on so many levels. I just had to do the work to create my new direction and redefine my identity. I had to be open to change. It needed to happen in order to lead me to where I was supposed to be: fulfilling my life's purpose.

As I mentioned earlier, as I began writing this book, I created a questionnaire and sent it out to a select group of people. The responses have allowed me to share with you real-life stories of major turning points. Jeannine is a woman with three kids who came to a major turning point in her life when she decided to divorce her husband. During her reassessment phase after the divorce, she describes realizing something very important. She writes, "My divorce was never about finding a better man, it was about finding a better me." I love the honesty of this statement and the recognition that it was about herself versus someone else. I also appreciate how she further expands on the experience: "When the divorce was final, I expected my life to suddenly, magically, be perfect. It wasn't. That hit like a ton of bricks. Getting the goods, it turns out, is only half the journey. You're not out of the woods yet. I wasn't anywhere close to the other side; where — or what — I wanted to be. Joseph Campbell says when you're in one place in your life and you want to be in another, there's an obstacle in your path. The thing to do, he says, is to identify the obstacle and turn it into an opening. 'The means for ascension,' he called it. Therapists call it a re-frame, a change of perspective and approach." I love the power of this idea.

Another great observation about the reassessment stage comes from Chad. I mentioned Chad and his father in earlier chapters. In my questionnaire I asked what tools or skills were gained from their "all is lost" experience. Chad responded, "That is a wonderful question and I think I can respond with a simple answer. I had to learn the tools of becoming a professional human being. I learned how to work on myself first, and my results and others will follow. Change is an inside/out job. The only short cut is focusing on becoming a better you by gaining conscious awareness of who you are and what you came to planet earth to fulfill."

These are powerful ideas that I want you to remember as you reassess your own situation. You are doing this only for you, no one else. The work you are doing is focused on the idea of you becoming active in your life and not repeating past patterns in the future. This is what will lead you toward personal growth. It will also help you to move forward instead of backward after any future fall or "all is lost" moment. You can become the active hero in your story; in order to do so, you have to do the emotional work so that, moving forward, you take action toward a new goal with a stronger sense of personal awareness.

Research

The next action I want you to take is to research what you want to do next. After you've taken the time to heal from the loss, think about the idea of your next goal. How can you take all the value that came from hitting rock bottom and use it as fuel toward what you're going to do next? As part of this research phase, I want you to identify a specific goal and then read every book, blog, and article you can get your hands on about people who are where you want to be.

When you identify a goal, then it just becomes about the process of mapping your way to it. You can do it. When you read about the stories of others or speak with others who are where you want to be, you gain insight on what path you can pave to get there. It is all about the journey. Be in the beauty of the process. There is so much to gain by being totally present in the research phase of planning your roadmap.

At the early stage of my research phase I found the book *Starting Your Own Consultancy* by Alan Weiss, founder of Summit Consulting Group. I connected to Alan's story of losing his job at the VP level when a new regime came in, and I became inspired by how he went on to create a seven-figure business out of his home. I thought, "I want to do that!" I ended up buying four more of Alan's books from his website. They really set the foundation for my business. He speaks to the reader in a very direct and logical way. Another tremendous book for entrepreneurs is *The E-Myth* by Michael E. Gerber, a no-nonsense book that gives you the straight facts about why a majority of small businesses fail and what you can do to make sure yours survives. He offers some pivotal information that will make a difference in the success of your business.

I also did loads of research on how to market my business. After being in the entertainment industry for seventeen years, I had a large Rolodex of contacts. I knew that writing a newsletter was one way that I'd get the word out. I had joined Facebook, which was relatively new in October of 2007, a time I was deep in the research phase of starting my own business. Facebook, Twitter, and LinkedIn have played a huge factor in the growth and success of my business. If you are thinking of starting your own business, you will want to read up on the value of social media. An excellent book on this subject is called *Crush It! Why NOW Is The Time To Cash In On Your Passion* by Gary Vaynerchuk. It will give you an overview of several of the social media outlets and how they can help you get ahead. I would also recommend Constant Contact, a great tool for sending out information through monthly newsletters and for informing your audience about events.

Evaluate Your Internal Motivations

When you prepare for your new chapter or your new story, you have to do the internal as well as the external work to get where you want to go. The key is making sure that your internal motivations for wanting the external goal are in alignment with the goal itself. When you strengthen your resolve from the inside, you increase your chances of attaining the external rewards. It's about mentally and emotionally preparing for the change and setting forth an intention from the inside.

These are some of the books I've read and loved over the last few years that have really contributed to my external success by doing the internal work: *The Millionaire Messenger* by Brendon Burchard, *The Power of Now* by Eckhart Tolle, *A New Earth* by Eckhart Tolle, *Linchpin: Are You Indispensable?* by Seth Godin, *Awaken The Giant Within* by Tony Robbins, *The War of Art* by Steven Pressfield, *On Becoming Fearless* by Arianna Huffington, *Get Out Of Your Own Way: The Five Keys To Surpassing Everyone's Expectations* by Robert K. Cooper, *Drive: The Surprising Truth About What Motivates Us* by Daniel H. Pink, *Maximum Achievement* by Brian Tracy, and one of my absolute favorites, *The Tools: Transform Problems Into Courage, Confidence and Creativity* by Phil Stutz and Barry Michels. I refer to these authors as members of my "circle of light."

All of the above were guides along my path to success. They informed, motivated, and inspired me to believe in the strength of my path. We cannot do it alone. It's all right to do the research and seek out the advice of others. Learning from others only strengthens and empowers us. By doing the emotional and mental work, you can attain any goal you set your mind to. You just have to do the research and the preparation internally and externally. There are no shortcuts.

As you think about your external goal, I want you to look at your internal motivations for wanting to achieve the goal. What do you hope to gain on a spiritual level from the external outcome? Is there a way that the achievement of your goal can involve giving to the betterment of others? When you think about this, imagine how you can contribute to others as a result of your accomplishment. As life goes on, I believe we evolve in a way where the importance of feeling true fulfillment comes from our ability to inspire others in the process. Do you believe in the power of your message to inspire others? Are you clear about what you want to say as a result of the experience? Does the external experience of the achievement of your goal support your internal motivations?

Define Your Goal

As I mentioned at the beginning of the chapter, when a central character hits the "all is lost" moment in a story, it is then followed by an "aha!" moment in which they finally realize what they need to do to achieve the goal. It is suddenly clear. With clarity you can define and focus on more of what you want. By looking at your story, you can learn from the obstacles you faced that led you to the point of no return. In the process, it often shines a light on what you don't want, but this helps you further define what you do want.

I believe the reason most writers have such difficulty defining what their character wants both internally and externally is because they don't have a clear sense of what they want in their own lives. If we don't know what we want in our own lives, then reflecting on it in the life of another can be challenging; however, the beauty and the gift of writing a story with fictional elements is that you get to imagine that your character has complete clarity, even if you don't. This is exactly where your imagination comes in. Your character can take on a side of you that might not be completely active in your own life; regardless, a quality you may not possess can take on a life of its own on the page. So try to apply this to the new story you are writing for yourself. Tap into a side of yourself that maybe isn't completely active yet and make it active on the page. It may awaken something inside you.

As I've discussed earlier, in my own life and the lives of millions of others, having biological children is a big dream to let go of. It is like the death of a life goal that was set since childhood. There are a lot of emotions that surface with the admission of this. I always visualized myself as being a mother. Yet, more important to me was finding the right person to have this experience with. I knew that I did not want to be a mom just to be a mom. I wanted to be a mom because it was a reflection of the love and commitment to someone I was deeply in love with. It had to stem from a true partnership. Yet, so far, this has not been a part of my destiny. I mourn the loss of this life experience; however, I made a promise to myself that the only way I would have a child is if I met someone who I could truly see being a partner in this destiny. Since this has not happened, I will say that shedding this desire for motherhood has been a journey. I know this is a journey for all of us who are going through it. When we let go of it, there is actually a sense of freedom that washes over us. We can embrace life and just know that our picture is going to look differently than what we initially imagined it to be. This is all right. We just have to redefine our destiny. We can find just as much beauty and fulfillment; it will just appear in different forms.

By letting go of one goal, I think it's important to define a new one. For me, I recognized that I could have the same "mothering" and "nurturing" type of experience with my clients. While working at the studio, I felt like my shows were my kids. I was lucky enough to be a part of the process of seeing them grow from a pilot into a television series that could possibly go on to enjoy tremendous success. I found this experience to be tremendously fulfilling on many levels. Now, in my own business, the writers I work with are like my kids. I want to see them all grow in their talent, succeed, and flourish on every level, both in their personal lives and in their careers.

After leaving the studio and taking the time to process my turn, I was able to define a clear goal. My goal is to teach story on a personal level and stop isolation by creating community through the power of sharing story. I don't want it to be limited to the entertainment business. I want to expand into the business market. I believe that knowing how to tell your story is the key to your success in every walk of life. It took a lot of work to come into this clarity, but it was worth doing the work. It gave me a new destiny that I was working toward. By knowing where I wanted to go and what I wanted to create, all I had to do was figure out how to get there.

Be An Active Hero

Now that you've taken the time to reassess, research, evaluate, and define your goal, it's time to be an active hero in your destiny. Being active is the most important step to take when hitting an "all is lost" moment. If you are writing your story in the way that you want your life to look from this point forward, write about the actions you want to see the central character (i.e., you!) take. You've clearly identified your goal. Now it's about thinking of the actions you will need to take to get to your destination.

With fiction, I tell writers that after the external goal has been clearly established in their story, we the audience should feel the pursuit of the goal in every scene. Actually, this applies to your life as well. Every day you should be taking small actions to move toward accomplishing your goal. No action is too small if it is something that links to your goal.

When I started my business, I organized my day so that I had time to market and promote my business, time to read scripts for my consults, time to answer all of my e-mails, time to take meetings, and time to reflect on my day and figure out what more I could do to grow and expand my business. When I started writing books, I had to organize my day to make time for this as well. I knew these were actions that I wanted to take because they moved me toward achieving my goal of teaching story on a global level and stopping isolation through building community by getting people to share their stories.

If I can do it, you can do it. Be clear on what actions, big or small, you can take that will get you closer to your external goal. By doing something productive in response to a major turning point, you may find that you will go in a direction that is actually more authentic to yourself than the one you started in. After we have our piece of humble pie, we see the world differently. After we move from our ego to our spirit, the world opens up in ways that we never imagined.

As part of my questionnaire I also asked, "What parts of your story do you feel can inspire and teach others how to make it through a turning point and move in a more authentic direction?" Howard answered, "All of the above...that is what we do as speakers, trainers, and educators. I've learned to 'see' with spiritual eyes as I lost the ability to see with physical eyes, but in the process I have learned to live with purpose." When we live with purpose, the world opens up in ways that we never thought possible. When this happens, our level of spiritual fulfillment deepens. We need to learn to move from ego to spirit, and then to the part of our journey where contributing to the greater good through accomplishing our goals comes into clear focus. When we help others, it fulfills our purpose in the process. When we are active in our destiny, we increase the chances of it coming to fruition. We all deserve to have our story reflect a fulfilled and happy life. This should be our mission at all times.

Remember: Your "all is lost" moment can lead to a renewed sense of purpose. It all comes down to your willingness to reassess, research, evaluate, define your goal, and then be an active hero in your destiny. This is your story. You want to make it the best it can be. You want to reflect on your life and know that you fulfilled your potential. You deserve to have your story reflect your truth. Truth is revealed when you hit rock bottom. By connecting to your truth, you learn that you can accomplish whatever your mind and heart set out to do. Your "all is lost" moment can be the trigger to a brighter future. It is all up to you to hear the message, be open to its meaning, and make it happen.

Exercise Eight

What is one "all is lost" moment that you faced in the past? What was the message that you felt coming through this experience? In your new story, describe how hitting this moment helped you to better understand what you had to do to attain your goal.

CHAPTER NINE

Reaching Your Goal

You Did It Before, You Can Do It Again

Many of us spend our lives searching for success when it is usually so close that we can reach out and touch it.

— *Russell H. Conwell*

If you achieve a monumental goal once, you can do it again. Your past is like a blueprint for you to use in mapping your way to your next goal. It also serves as a reminder of what works and what does not work when you pursue your next goal. I remember the day I received the call that I got the job with a big studio. It was a culmination of thirteen years of effort from the time I was an assistant to the time I got the corner office on the well-known studio lot. I was going to be Vice President of Current Programs. During those thirteen years, I recalled every obstacle I had to move through to get there. I grew so much during that time. I kept my focus on the end goal. I faced many obstacles along the way. I didn't let them knock me off track. My moment had arrived. I had achieved my goal. I had worked tooth and nail for it. I felt exhilarated. Of course, it meant having to leave my mentor, Aaron Spelling, and the nest that led to my growth as an executive. I knew that I was ready. It was my time. There is no greater feeling than returning to this moment and recognizing that if I was able to achieve something at this level before, I could do it again.

Think of how you felt during your huge life achievements. Draw from these emotions and memories. Think about the lessons learned along the way. In fiction, the way that you see how the old influences the new goal is by looking at who your central character is when the story starts and who they are when the story ends. You think about what they wanted in the beginning and why they wanted it. Did this change by the end? Did your character change in the process?

In the movie *Silver Linings Playbook*, screenplay written by David O. Russell from the novel written by Matthew Quick, the protagonist Pat (Bradley Cooper) has lost his house and his wife and has just spent eight months in an out-of-state institution. He is determined to see his wife again despite the things she did that led to this series of downward-spiraling events in his life. Pat hits all kinds of obstacles on the way to this goal. He meets Tiffany (Jennifer Lawrence), a rebellious girl who offers to design a way for Pat to see his wife. They work together on a dance competition at which his wife will be present. During the process of working with Tiffany on the dance, however, something transforms in Pat. He sees the effort that Tiffany puts into helping him achieve his goal. When he ultimately does see his wife at the dance, he has a completely different reaction than he had anticipated. He moves from an initial goal of ego to a new goal of spirit.

This demonstrates how in your story you can start off thinking that you want to accomplish the external goal for one reason. Then, through the process of hitting obstacles on your way to that goal, you may discover that your internal motivation shifts for the external outcome that you desire. Your goal may not change. However, your reason for wanting to attain the goal may change. *You* change. This is where you will see your own growth as a protagonist in your story.

By better understanding your internal motivations, you will be able to move toward a more positive outcome in your own story. These steps will help to inform the choices you make on the way toward your external goal. There are four important things you can do to help you understand your internal motivations for what you hope to gain externally from achieving your goals:

- Redirection
- Reflection
- Recognition
- Response

Redirection

When I talk about redirection, I simply mean the ability to change focus, perspective, or strategy to reach your goal. By redirecting how you set your new goal and how you view your past achievements, you can produce a stronger outcome in your achievement of the current goal. One way to redirect is to better align your internal desire with the external accomplishment you are seeking. This is a tool that I've acquired and is commonly used in fiction. Usually, a story starts with the hero being driven toward the goal for ego-related motivations. By hitting hurdles, the central character is able to see that maybe her philosophy behind her pursuit isn't serving her. She realizes that there is something out of sync between her internal desire and the external outcome. This is when character growth happens. She is able to change her philosophy and redirect her strategy so that she can accomplish her goal. You can do the same thing in your life and with the pursuit of your goal. When you first identify your external goal, recognize that your reasons for wanting to achieve it may need to grow from ego to spirit. This is all right. You can redirect your focus. This is part of your journey. It is what makes your story compelling. Your growth is what makes us root for you to accomplish your goal. If you can learn the technique of redirecting and aligning your internal desire with your external goal, you increase the chances of achieving your goal and being fulfilled by it.

Your history of reaching changing goals is a valuable tool for you to utilize in the pursuit of your new goal. By looking at the way you made choices in the past and the outcomes that they led to, you will be able to make stronger choices in your new story that will lead you to your new goal. You need to redirect how you view some of your past accomplishments in order to achieve stronger results with your new goals. When you think about all that you've achieved in your life, know that if you've done it before, you can do it again. Reaching goals is a huge part of your life, from the time you're born to the time you leave the nest. You need to learn to revisit these moments and remember exactly what it felt like to experience the accomplishment of the goal. Upon revisiting your past accomplishments, you will see that by redirecting the way you view them, you will get stronger results in the future.

When you reach a goal and truly feel the magnitude of the outcome, it's most likely that your internal desire is in tune with the external reward. On the other hand, when you attain a certain goal and the external reward does not reach your internal expectation, you need to redirect your expectations of the outcome. Maybe you were hoping for some shift to happen on the inside, or maybe your external goal wasn't the best choice to fulfill your internal intention. You often have to learn what doesn't work before you learn what does.

There is no better feeling than setting a goal and attaining it. If you are active in your destiny, you are setting goals on a daily basis. You are taking action toward the achievement of your goals and you are an active hero in your own story. You know what it takes to set a goal and make it happen. If somewhere along the line you become inactive in the pursuit of your destiny, you have to consider what is causing your loss of momentum. You may get stuck. Your desire may dwindle. If you are not moving forward, it is because something is blocking your ability. If you think about what is stopping you, it is often due to fear or a number of other emotions caused by a build-up of past wounds from past experiences where the results were not as great as you hoped they would be. By processing the wound and redirecting how you see it, you can learn to use it to fuel you forward and move you closer to your destiny.

One wound may stem from your loss of desire to go in a certain direction. In my own life, after going through a number of relationships that didn't work out, I began to lose my desire to want a relationship. I redirected my focus and threw myself into my work. My work fulfilled me. My work felt safe. My work gave me the results I wanted. My work was consistent. Desire for romantic love took a hiatus; it left my life for a long period of time. There were moments when I truly wondered if it would return. Lately, I feel closer to the possibility. There is an energy that is waking me up and helping me to believe again. I am experiencing a rare connection. It is a gift. After setting the foundation for my business and accomplishing some monumental goals along the way, I feel as if I am ready to welcome this energy back into my life. It has given me hope that it is ready to return. This time, I am ready to embrace it. I've learned how to use my past wound as fuel to drive me forward in my pursuit.

Redirecting the way you view your wounds will change your story and change your life. In fiction, I teach my writers the idea that their central character has a wound that drives them and a flaw that gets in their way. I ask writers to determine what those wounds and flaws are. Wounds can drive you forward. Wounds also give you information. They are often caused by isolated moments in your life where your actions didn't lead you to the experience you intended. You may get into a situation with good intentions, but soon discover that it wasn't meant to be. You have to go in another direction. You have to pick yourself up and figure out a stronger path. When you think about why certain things don't work out, it might help you to look at your internal motivations that fueled what you hoped for the external outcome.

By looking back at all the goals you have accomplished in your life up to this point, you can learn to draw from that momentum and create new goals that may bring you even more satisfaction. You can heighten your satisfaction in reaching these goals by understanding that your motivations for wanting to achieve a goal can change as you evolve. As you grow older, you begin to see that your accomplishments can be about more than just your personal satisfaction. They can contribute to the greater good. By simply redirecting the way you see your new goal, you can put things in proper alignment with inner values and lead yourself to stronger results. When your motivations evolve, you step into a higher consciousness where your goals, and your reasons for wanting to attain them, become about so much more.

Reflection

Think back to your childhood and reflect on the emotions involved in attaining your early goals. Recall these early life moments and the type of rewards that came with them. What did it make you want to do? For many of us, it began the process of wanting to do more so that you could receive more validation for your actions. I love observing one of my best friends, Melinda, with her two children, Kate and Alex. Melinda is an incredible mother. She is also a senior-level executive at a studio. I see her walk the balance between giving her kids emotional rewards and setting boundaries for what is not all right. For example, if Kate is whining, Melinda might say, "Choose your words Kate; whining doesn't work." I love this. She makes it clear to Kate what is not working and what would work if she just applies herself. Kate wants to make her mom happy, so she works toward the goal of expressing herself in a better way. Childhood is where it all begins.

As a kid, I was never a straight-A student. I always felt that my older brother, Mike, had it easier when it came to grades. I desired the external reward that came with getting an A; I just often was in conflict about doing the internal work to get there. I think my focus was also a little more involved in my social life. So I had to learn discipline to do the work to get the grades that made my parents happy and moved me to the next level. I had to learn that my internal motivations for wanting the grades had to be honed in order to receive the grades that would bring the external rewards. My younger sister was also a very strong student. She did the work and the grades were the result. I think that she had a stronger understanding of how to balance her academic and social life through watching my brother and me. Today my brother is a dentist and my sister is an attorney. Our parents' expectations and our desire to fulfill those expectations are what led to each of us fulfilling our destiny.

Graduation from school is the next life moment you can look back on and see how a series of actions led to a specific destination. For most of us, I'd say that the external experience of graduation did align with our internal expectations. Through achieving a series of small goals, we got good grades that led to a bigger outcome: graduation. Graduation from any level of education is a very big life moment. Try reflecting on all the times you've graduated in your life. I think I have a clear memory of all my pinnacle graduations. They were amongst the highest moments of joy I have experienced in my life.

I remember my graduation from USC the most. First off, college is such a wild experience. You have to learn balance and time management while learning how to structure your social life and academic life. You go through the "little fish in a big ocean" experience. But quickly you figure out your place in the ocean. How do you have value when the scope seems so much bigger than what we knew? There is so much growth involved at this point in life. I definitely recall moments when my social life outweighed my educational responsibilities. When I would receive grades I knew were not up to the standards that my parents expected, I would do whatever I needed to do to get back on track. USC is not a cheap school. My father told me that if I graduated in four years, I could do whatever I wanted in my life. He just wanted me to graduate. This gave me the sense that if I accomplished this task and reached his expectation in the process, freedom of choice would follow. This was a huge motivator for me. So when I did everything I needed to do to make this dream a reality, and graduation was the external reward, there was no greater feeling.

As you evolve, you need to have a strong inner barometer for what feels right and what does not. Hopefully you learn from your mistakes about what not to do and what doesn't work. Your missteps have tremendous value in your direction. They may feel more like bumps when you hit them, but when you reflect back you will see them as gifts that helped nudge you in a stronger direction.

When it comes to love, we also set goals for ourselves. When we were young, I think most of us had different expectations of what our lives would look like versus how they turned out. You conjure up a picture. You think about the "happily ever after" moment that you are sure is part of your destiny and you imagine how you will be in this picture. When I think about my generation versus my parents' generation, the goal of marriage does not carry the same kind of weight as before. In my generation, I feel that women want more than just marriage. We want a career and something to fulfill us in addition to family. My mom went back to law school at age 39. This taught me the importance of recognizing your needs; if you wanted more, than you had to go after it and create it, and it was never too late.

I remember thinking that by age 25 I'd be married with one kid and more on the way. When I reached 25, I knew I was not ready for this goal. There was so much I wanted to do with my life. Also, I had not met the guy that I could imagine sharing this kind of picture with. So I chose to pursue the professional side of my life and see at what point the personal side developed. I did wind up meeting my now ex-husband at age 26 and marrying him at age 31. So, in one way, I did fulfill a personal goal around the time parameter I had set for myself. However, I think the setting of this goal and the attainment of it was motivated by the wrong internal motivations. I would not really be able to see this until after it ended.

The mistakes you make along your quest for a goal are not in vain; they will help you better understand what works and what does not work. I love a quote by Maya Angelou, which Oprah Winfrey has used often in her career: "When you know better, you do better." I cannot begin to tell you how much I love these words. They allow a burden to be lifted off our shoulders when we think about the shame we attach to certain moments in our lives. Maybe the only reason we did something the wrong way was because we still needed to learn how to do it right. The obstacle was set in our way because there were still things we needed to discover about what was the right direction for us.

When you go through life turning points like divorce and betrayal, you can become paralyzed in your quest to go after future goals in your personal life. You may turn your attention toward the attainment of professional goals because you feel safer in this arena. Professional achievement may come easier because it doesn't involve as many personal emotions. I think you are often trained better in the professional world. You have more opportunity to see what works and what doesn't work. I think that many of us feel more comfortable in the office than we do at home. This becomes evident as you see more and more people choose to stay in the office later and later. I saw this happen a lot in the industry to the people around me. It made me reflect on being more careful with the choices I made when it came to love.

If you want to achieve your personal goals again and learn to be an active hero in your new story, you need to wake up to the idea that there are internal desires behind the external outcomes. If you reflect on where you've been and what hasn't worked, you can figure out how to hone your internal motivations to be a better match with your external goals. When you change from the inside, there will be greater rewards on the outside.

Take an honest look at your motivations for wanting to achieve your new goal, and apply the idea of moving from ego to spirit. When you are operating from your spirit, connecting the greater good with the achievement of your goal becomes more evident. With this, you move to a higher place of being. You discover new reasons to set new goals. As you reflect on your past motivations, you'll gain insights into where you were emotionally in your life during the achievement (or not) of past goals. You can also begin to see that your internal life has evolved and that maybe it's time that your external goals reflect your evolving internal motivations.

Recognition

Recognition is both an internal and external experience. Validation is part of this. While in school, you get recognition from your teachers and your parents for the grades you get. When you do a good job at work, you may receive a bonus, a higher salary, or a change in title. In your personal life, recognition comes in response to the actions taken. You may move in with a partner, get engaged, get married, and commit to the possibility of creating a "happily ever after" experience. All these forms of recognition set the bar for certain accomplishments. They make you want to achieve.

You may seek the above kinds of recognition and when you experience it, you discover that it wasn't quite what you thought it would be. You had a fantasy that when you got married or you received a certain promotion, the world would open up and life would take you to new heights. When this doesn't happen the way you may have envisioned it, you have to learn to do the internal work and look within to find what you hoped for externally. The recognition you've been conditioned to seek on the outside, learn to find it within. You can learn to give yourself rewards and recognition. When you find internal balance, the external experience will deepen in meaning.

As you progress in life, you evolve. Events and achievements carry a deeper meaning for you. In the beginning, recognition often comes from the ego. You find your perfect mate so you can create the perfect picture and have everyone else think that you have it all. You strive to achieve at your job so that you get the perfect title, the high salary, and the corner office so that, from the outside looking in, you appear to have it all together. You paint the picture of the life that you are conditioned and socialized to believe would be the answer to your happiness. You are often too busy thinking about what the picture will look like from the outside looking in that you fail to consider what it will look like from the inside looking out.

When you learn to value your internal experience more than the external, you change and transcend. Think about this in your life and in your new story. You see that how you experience the external situations from the inside carries so much more significance than how the outside experience appears to others. You discover what makes you happy by seeing how things truly make you feel. As you fine-tune this awareness, your outer quest may turn inward. You might start doing yoga, meditation, volunteering, seeking spiritual guidance, following through, showing up and being present. By doing these things, you can see that these are the experiences that define your character and bring you happiness from the inside. This gives the external rewards less importance.

In the entertainment industry, I have worked with people who have attained enormous amounts of wealth simply by writing stories. The weight of their words had more and more value as they learned the tools of what to do and how to do it well. Their shows sold, their series succeeded, the rewards came in leaps and bounds. Do I think they became happier in the process? Very often, I found that this was not the case. In fact, sometimes it was the exact opposite. They fantasized back to the times when they were hungry and they put true happiness on the quest versus the destination. The more they gained, the more they had to lose if the accomplishments weren't always hitting the standard they needed to hit to maintain the external picture of success. This is so true for so many people. On our quest for having it all, in the antiquated way we've been socialized to go after it, we are losing our sense of self and everything we achieve seems to come at a cost to something else.

Once you recognize this truth, you begin to really move from your ego to your spirit. You see that the external experience does not fulfill the internal desire. You see that the beauty of life is in the journey much more than the destination. What this does from an internal place is it motivates us to be in the present. It helps you to see that you need to stop pursuing the external outcome in hopes of recognition; instead, you need to focus on being present in the moment and appreciating the beauty of what is. For some of you, this recognition comes earlier in life. It all depends on your turning points. The more of these you go through, the more awake you become to what you have in front of you. Your path humbles your growth. You begin to recognize that there is a gift in going the wrong way. It might actually bring you to a brighter destination if you evolve with the experience and become more conscious of your spirit in the process.

After leaving the world of being a VP and a studio executive, I remember that it was a huge transition to shed the identity of who I was. I had to really learn to do the internal work to recognize that my worth and my identity was going to come from a different source now. I was leaving the security of the picture I had painted for seventeen years and moving into the unknown. Part of this transition was taking a pay cut the first two years. By the third year, I was earning something comparable to what I had made in the executive world; however, I had accrued more debt along the way. What I came to recognize was that going after a dream on my own terms was going to cost. It did in the beginning. Then, when I surpassed my previous income, it made it all worth the effort.

Another part of this transition of going out on my own was that I had to learn to paint a new picture not connected to the external title or rewards, but instead to how the work made me feel from the inside. I knew that once I shifted the focus and created a business based on everything that I loved to do that the external reward would follow. It did. What I found was that I was ready for the internal recognition that came with this life passage. You are so much more than the title you hold. Your value comes in your actions and how you make others feel and how it makes you feel in the process.

Response

When you respond, you are active. By doing the work and better understanding your internal desires, you will be able to make better choices in how to respond. I believe that most of what you seek on the outside, you can find within. You just have to do the emotional work. When you do, you evolve and begin to see that there is greater value in learning to respond from your spirit versus your ego on the way to the goal. Your ego does serve a purpose in the beginning. It helps you to identify what you want so that you know how to respond. Then, it evolves. The rewards are all there. You have to learn to be open to the message. You have to start measuring your sense of worth from the actions taken that bring a stronger reward from the inside and from the gratitude you feel, not the things you attain.

Response in fiction is all about taking action. In a script, with each action taken by the central character toward the pursuit of a goal, I ask writers to think about the following: What is the action taken, what is the obstacle hit, and what is the reminder of the external/internal stakes if the goal is not achieved? For each action taken, I tell them to think about all of these steps. I want you to do this when writing your new story the way you want your life to play out. For each goal that you set, think about the obstacles you may run into and the impact on your life if you do not achieve your goal. Envision yourself getting over each obstacle. If you didn't learn from your parents that you are capable of achieving anything you set your mind to, learn it from yourself. You can do it. By responding to your life, you set things in motion and you move closer toward your destiny.

In the movie *Argo*, written by Chris Terrio, we see what happens when the lead character Tony Mendez (Ben Affleck) responds to a dilemma. The dilemma is that Americans were taken hostage in Iran and that six of them managed to escape to the official residence of a Canadian Ambassador. Mendez's response is to make a plan to manufacture a fake movie production so that he can get his people in there to save the escapees. The goal, and the action needed toward that goal, is clear. They hit many escalating obstacles, but the goal is always in clear view. The stakes continue to escalate. There is a ticking clock that adds to the suspense of the outcome. We root for the goal to be achieved. We feel the growth of the characters involved. All of the action that takes place in this movie is moving toward the goal of getting the six escaped hostages safely out of Iran. It's clear, we identify, and we become emotionally invested.

It is through taking action and hitting obstacles that you begin to connect with your spirit. The obstacles are put in your path to move you toward a higher place of being while moving through your journey. As you evolve, you recognize when you're responding from the spirit and when you're responding from the ego. This awareness is a daily practice. In any well-written story, you see that the central character initially wants to achieve the external goal for ego-related reasons. Then, after hitting obstacles, he/she begins to move into the spirit. By responding from the spirit, the central character may even begin to see how the achievement of their goal could benefit the greater good. They evolve and transcend. They move to a higher place of being. We do that in our lives as well; some of us are aware of it, while others of us are not. You may believe you move to a higher level of consciousness, and once you hit this level, you can stay there. Actually, the practice of keeping a balance between the ego and the spirit is something you do on a daily basis. How you respond to any given situation determines the outcome. Like anything in life, the more you practice, the better you become at it. So, when you respond by taking action, or by your reaction to any given situation, learn the gift of embracing the spirit versus fueling the ego.

The way you respond to things in life is what determines your character on many levels. In fiction writing, action reveals character and the words you use reveal character. When you respond from the spirit, you come from a deeper place of awareness in any given situation. When you come from this place of higher consciousness, the external goal will have a stronger internal reward. You begin to understand the true value of your internal world. When you achieve one of your goals, you feel your own growth from where you started to where you ended. You can look at your reactions from the past and learn how to react or respond in the future. Your responses are actions you take that can lead you to your destiny and fulfill your calling or life's purpose. When you move into your spirit, your calling beckons you. You are more open to hearing the sound of its voice. Whether you move toward it or away from it is up to you.

When you take the time to redirect, reflect, and think about acts of recognition and response in your life up to this point, you can see where you were, where you are now, and where you want to go. You can learn from your old story and create the type of new story you want for your life. You can evolve into seeing the worth of your internal world and you can do the work it takes on a daily basis to choose the spirit over the ego in any given situation. By choosing the spirit, you increase your chances of finding greater fulfillment from pursuing your goals and achieving them. When you learn that you can move from ego to spirit to the greater good when it comes to the goals you set for yourself, you add depth to the way that you experience your goals and your life.

Exercise Nine

What is the external goal for your new story? How can you better align your internal and external motivations to help make the attainment of your goal as internally fulfilling as possible?

CHAPTER TEN

Your New Story

Everyone thinks of changing the world, but no one thinks of changing himself.
— *Leo Tolstoy*

The way you write your new story can change your life. It all comes down to the goals you set and the actions you take. I was inspired to write this book because of the value I discovered in changing my own story and life after hitting an unexpected turning point. After hitting rock bottom, I connected with my spirit in a stronger way than I ever imagined. I suddenly was able to see things more clearly. A door opened up. My world as I knew it changed. Through focused action I created a company that reflected everything I love to do, at the core of which is helping people. I love working with people on their stories and showing them how to connect their life moments with their story in a way that will bring them the greatest value. Story is the universal element that connects people on all levels. Knowing how to tell your story can lead you to tremendous wealth on a physical, emotional, and spiritual level.

If you do the emotional work, you will increase your chances of success. I am always doing the emotional work to stay connected to my own story and to understand myself on a deeper level. When I am in life moments where I feel my wounds resurface, I think back to the origin of the wound and try to understand why I am still letting this past experience affect me. I am committed to the idea of creating change through our stories. I know that by learning how to apply the story tools that I've acquired over my career and gone over in this book, I've been able to create monumental change in my life. I want you to be able to do the same. I understand your pain. I know what it's like to feel that you have been denied arrival to your planned destination. I also know what it's like to have to pick yourself up after a fall and redefine a new path. What I've found is that your new path can be more authentic than the original one you set out on. By writing summary lines and charting story arcs for your own life story, you will paint the picture of the new life you are going to create. The key to all of it is defining what you want, understanding the internal and external aspects of your desire, creating a plan, putting your plan into action, looking at your obstacles as steps toward your destiny versus steps away from it, and knowing that you can achieve your goal and move from ego to spirit in the process. You are the author of your life. You have the creative ability to design your life the way that you want it to look. It all comes down to answering a question that is both simple and complex: What do you want the story of your life to be?

Start by thinking about the intentions behind your story. Do you want to create change personally, professionally, or both? Do you want to better understand how to blend your personal and your professional lives so that you are no longer in conflict between the two? What do you want? Think about this from an internal and external perspective. By understanding what you want your end result to be and going into your story with strong intentions, you will increase your chances of being fulfilled by the outcome. When you fail to do the emotional work, your vision of happiness can be clouded. It may not be the best picture for you. This is why it is so important to do the work we've discussed so that you can write your new story from a healthy state of being.

Let's recap how you can change your story. First, you begin to view your turning points and "all is lost" moments as signs that there's a stronger direction for you to go toward. You begin to see the value in hitting obstacles and recognize that they can move you forward instead of hold you back. You begin to see yourself as the active hero in your own story versus the victim who never recovers from the wound. You take small actions that lead to a bigger destination. You commit to your own possibility.

Here are five factors that play an important role in changing your story:

- Hitting rock bottom
- Defining what you want both externally and internally
- Becoming the hero in your own story
- Facing fear
- Evolving to a higher consciousness

Hitting Rock Bottom

My hope is that now you are able to view your moments of hitting rock bottom in a stronger way. When you hit rock bottom, there is clearly nowhere to go but up. Hitting rock bottom reminds you of the stakes that are involved if you don't change your story. When you hit rock bottom, you are often saying goodbye to one way of life while learning to be open to your new possibility. You are redefining your own "happily ever after." To quote J.K. Rowling, author of the *Harry Potter* novels, "Rock bottom became the foundation upon which I rebuilt my life."

With the experience of hitting rock bottom, you begin to see the value of rebuilding your life. You may have been standing on a faulty foundation all along but you didn't realize it until that bottom fell out from under you. This gives you a new opportunity to build a new foundation. Only this time the hope is that you will be smarter in the materials or the people you choose to rebuild with.

Defining What You Want Both Externally And Internally

In fiction, as I've mentioned many times throughout this book, when the central character hits rock bottom, it's on the way to achieving an external goal that has already been set. When you hit rock bottom in real life, it could happen on the path to an external goal or it could happen after reaching the goal. Basically this means that after hitting rock bottom, you need to set a new goal. Before you get to that point, though, you need to define what it is that you want both externally and internally. After reading this book, I hope that you have a stronger sense of the importance of putting these two desires into alignment; in other words, what you want on the inside has to be in accord with what you want on the outside. What will also play a part in defining your new goal is considering how your new direction can not only benefit you, but also can, in some way, benefit the greater good.

Start with the external outcome you desire. After your turning point, what do you want to make happen externally in your life? Do you want a new job? Do you want to fall in love? Do you want to buy a house? Do you want to go on a trip around the world and soak up the cultures of other regions? Do you want to write a book so that the experience you went through has value and could be used in a way that will affect the masses? Do you want to know what it is to live alone? I want you to really think about what you want to experience in an external way for the next part of your story.

Next think about *why* you want what you want. How are you going to satiate your inner world? Hopefully by this point in your life you have come to the realization that all of the answers are within you. So understanding how to satisfy the hunger of your inner world in a healthy way needs to factor into your external pursuit. Think about yourself at the end of your new story. What are the emotions that you hope will come with the external journey? On this new path, you should have a new appreciation for the obstacles you will hit along the way. You should also write down what the stakes are if you don't attain the goal.

By defining what you want and writing it down, you are taking a gigantic step toward manifesting your destiny.

Becoming The Hero In Your Own Story

You are the author of your life. You are the hero in your story. You have two choices: You can be an active hero, or you can be a passive hero. You can be the type of person who makes things happen, or you can be the type of person who reacts to what happens to them. You can be in pursuit of your new goal on a daily basis, or you can remain stagnant. You can think about how the achievement of your goal can benefit you and the greater good in some way, or you can remain in your ego and think only of yourself. It all comes down to the choices you make.

Some of the most interesting heroes in fiction are also some of the most flawed and complex. Embrace your flaws. They contribute to your character. They add flavor. I think that flaws connect us to one another. They demonstrate that perfection does not exist. I think that we can all find comfort in this truth. In fiction, when we see a character say something self-deprecating when they feel unsure about something, it draws us to them. We want to know more about the wound that is driving this feeling because we may have a similar wound.

What kind of hero do you want to be in your story? What kind of pursuit do you desire to go after? What do you see being involved in your pursuit? What will allow others to connect with you? What is the wound that drives you and the flaw that gets in your way? Have fun with writing yourself as a character and seeing yourself in a new light. Recognize that you are the only protagonist in your story. It is only you who will lead you to your destiny.

When you commit to the recognition of your new role in your life, you can utilize this new state of being to help get you where you want to go. Think about the heroes and heroines in the stories that really resonate with you. What attributes do they have that you would like to have? Or maybe you do have similar attributes, but you just never knew how to put them to good use. Seeing yourself in this new role may help you to realize that there are no higher stakes than using the short time you have to make a difference in a real way. In order to make a difference, you have to learn to be active and learn the value of each goal that you set. Also, think about the growth that heroes go through. They may start out thinking that they want to achieve the goal for one reason, but through hitting obstacles and getting humbled they grow into the type of people who deserve the title of hero. You can do the same. There is no reason why you can't be an active hero in your own story. As long as you are alive, there is time to write a new story.

Also, I want you to think about the cycles that a hero goes through on their way to a goal. They often start in a place of loss where we empathize with them and root for them to achieve their goal. Part of being in a place of loss is being confronted with a dilemma. As I've explained, a dilemma is where neither choice is a good choice and neither choice is a clear choice. There are pluses and minuses to both sides. Once a character makes a choice, an external goal is set. Then they hit several obstacles on the way to their goal. Just when they think that they have it all figured out, they hit an "all is lost" moment. The gift of this moment, and by this point I hope you see it as a gift too, is that it shines the light from within and they figure out what they really want and how to get it. Finally, they are able to achieve the goal. So think about this cycle with each goal you set in your life that is leading you toward the greater picture that you want to create.

You are both the author and the hero of your story. You decide if it's going to be a story worth telling. You make the choices that lead you in your ultimate direction. The gift of failing and going in the wrong direction is that it helps you to see where you don't want to go and what you don't want to do. There is information to be gathered from your "failures." There are lessons to be absorbed. If you think of your life as a story, you know that there are always major obstacles on the way to any goal worth attaining. Now you also know that you can, in fact, get past the obstacles and attain the goal.

Facing Fear

Fear plays such a huge part in the pursuit of many goals. You need to understand how running away from your fear is not going to move you forward. What will move you forward is learning how to run toward fear and to move through it. Fear is often the emotion behind the internal obstacles we put in front of ourselves. Yet when we look at the core of our fear, we can see that the definition given to fear (i.e., "false evidence appearing real") is actually true. Fear is an internal obstacle that we need to understand how to use to our advantage instead of letting it get in the way of achieving our destiny.

When I launched my company in the middle of a writers' strike, my biggest fear was that the timing was wrong for the niche that I had created and that I wouldn't hear back from anyone. My concept was a fee-based service where writers hire me on a per-project basis. Knowing that writers were going to be under even more financial stress added to my own anxiety. On the day that I launched my website announcing my business, the fact that I received 175 email responses that first day and booked twenty meetings that first week told me that this was a strong sign of things to come. I knew going into it that I was jumping off one of the biggest cliffs of my life, but I faced it and went through with it despite my greatest fear, like a hero. When I saw that the fear had no power, I started to change my mind about how I treat fear in my life. I acknowledge its presence, but I don't give into it.

Another event that forced me to face my fear shortly after I opened my company involved a public speaking event. I was invited to Seattle to speak at the Northwestern Screenwriters Guild. It was a three-day event. The first night was a question and answer, which was a piece of cake. I loved it. The next morning I woke up and realized that this was the first event where I would be the only one speaking for about eight hours. I knew absolutely no one in the audience. The idea of this elated me and petrified me at the same time. When I got up to speak, my throat got dry and my heart started beating out of my chest. I felt fear. It felt as if someone had taken an eraser to my brain and erased the past seventeen years of knowledge that I had to share. What I did to help myself move past this fear was that I asked the audience to go around the room and have each participant introduce themselves and tell me why they were there. Suddenly, when I heard them speak, I felt as if I knew them. The fear disappeared. On the way home, I realized that I needed to get every book out there on public speaking. I could not believe that I had not thought of this. At that time I had a career's worth of knowledge to share, yet I had not purchased one book on presenting. This experience led me to Jerry Weissman's book, *Presenting To Win*. This is my go-to book. Jerry says that fear really comes when you are not prepared. When you are prepared in every way, the fear disappears. I read many other books on public speaking. One of my other favorites is *As We Speak* by Peter Meyers and Shann Nix. I also love the advice given by Brendon Burchard to speakers in *The Millionaire Messenger* and at his Expert Academy events. I now love public speaking. I am always waiting in anticipation for my next event. I love connecting with an audience over our shared passion for stories.

Moments like what I experienced in Seattle make you vulnerable, but also wake you up to your own fear. If you want to change, you have to be open to the work you need to do in order to get there. Facing your fears is part of this work. In your story, what are you most afraid of? What are your fears behind attaining the goals that you want to attain? What are those fears based on? When you take the time to move through what it is that is making you feel the fear, then you dilute its power.

You can use fear to your advantage if you think about it. What do you fear will happen if you don't write your life story in the way we want it to look? What if you leave this earth with a life unrealized? You can use this fear to drive you forward. Think about your story. Believe that you can be the kind of hero you want to be and you can face your fear with each obstacle that comes your way. You can move toward your fear and dissolve its effect on you. If you do this, then you will know what you are capable of achieving.

Evolving To a Higher Consciousness

When you are writing your new story, be aware of your own growth from start to finish. How are you going to evolve as the hero in your story? Think about the person you were before you hit certain pivotal life moments when your life took a turn. Think about the person that you are after the turning point. Countless people have told me that as devastating as some of their turning points have been, they feel that they are better people after having survived the turns. I believe that the reason for this is because we evolve as human beings. You move to a higher place when you face tragedy and you learn that your spirit can guide you through it. It wakes you up to the idea that time is precious. If you are not living the story you want to be living, then you need to take the time to reassess, rebuild, redefine, and start writing the story that you believe you deserve.

Numerous books that fell into my lap during the process of writing this book covered in one way or another the process of moving to a higher consciousness. These books included *The Tools: Transform Your Problems Into Courage, Confidence, and Creativity* by Phil Stutz and Barry Michels, *The New Human: Understanding Our Humanity and Embracing Our Divinity* by DeAnne Hampton, *Spiritual Solutions: Answers to Life's Greatest Challenges* by Deepak Chopra, *Turning Pro* by Steven Pressfield, *The Message: A Guide To Being Human* by LD Thompson, and *Wishes Fulfilled* by Dr. Wayne Dyer.

I give tremendous gratitude to these authors. The concept of moving into a higher consciousness fascinates me. It makes me think that the reason why this message is being sent to so many of us through words and our own experience is for us to continue delivering this message of a higher consciousness.

When we hit obstacles and we learn that we can get over them, we grow. When we are able to see that some of our beliefs and values are holding us back instead of moving us forward, we evolve. When we learn that it is better to respond from our spirit than from our ego, we mature. When we let go of thinking that starts with "I'll be happy when..." we free ourselves of the burden that comes with it. When we hit rock bottom and discover that the goal can still be achieved or that a new goal awaits us that points us in a more authentic direction that's in harmony with our spirit, we develop and move to a higher consciousness.

In Conclusion

By learning how to apply the story tools that I've given you, you can write your new story and change your life. When you write things down, you are making a declaration. By doing this you are committing to a journey. When you commit, you take action. When you take action, you produce results.

Your turning points in life have so much beauty in them. It often takes time to truly be able to see it, but when you do, you can see the gift. Recognize that your turns make your story one that is worth telling. Your falls make you human. They connect you with those you want to connect with. Your experience has tremendous value.

The tools I've given you are the same ones I've used in my own life to redefine, to reassess, and to change direction after my turning points. I did the work because I knew that there was so much more I wanted to accomplish. In choosing my new direction of running my own company, and defining my mission to stop isolation and create community through the sharing of our personal stories, I am moving in a more authentic direction. I now give gratitude to my turning points. I know that if I can do it, you can do it.

I encourage you to do the work and to recognize the power you hold in being the author of your own life. I want you to start thinking about all of the choices that you make, what is motivating them, and whether they are in alignment with the outcome you are seeking. Nourish your spirit. Understand your ego. You can become the active hero in your own story. You can write the new story that reflects the life you truly want. If you truly believe it, meditate on it, envision it, and take action, there is nothing that is stopping you from having the life you envision.

Exercise Ten

What will be the external rewards when you reach the goal in your new story? What will be the internal rewards? What are the stakes if the goal isn't achieved? Use these lists to motivate yourself daily toward the achievement of your goal.

ACKNOWLEDGMENTS

I FOUND MY INSPIRATION FOR WRITING THIS BOOK FROM SO MANY people, places and events. I consider the following people to be a part of my circle of light.

I would like to thank my family first and foremost. They are the glue that keeps me together. I feel very blessed having them as partners along on my life journey and for all that they do to add to my growth and my being. This includes my mom (who is and always will be my rock); my dad (who is my light), his girlfriend, Debra Harvey, and her son Derrin and his wife Ramie, and daughter Hope and son Cash; my brother (who has served as such a strong and positive role model), his wife Linda and my godson, Nicholas; and my sister (who is my kindred spirit) and her husband, Matt.

I would like to thank my editor and friend, Lili Ramirez. I love working with you. You get me. You know how to organize my thoughts and clarify my meaning. I am grateful for you and your gift.

To my publisher Michael Wiese and his wife Geraldine Overton, and his team including Ken Lee, Manny Otto, Bill Morosi, and Matt Barber. I would like to thank John Brenner for my beautiful cover. I love being a part of this family. You are all so special. Michael, you remind me of the spirit that Aaron Spelling had. I feel blessed for your belief in me and for the platform that you and your team provide. Geraldine, your notes elevated my book to a whole new level. Matt, your incredible notes and support were invaluable.

I would like to thank my inner circle of friends. Your friendship adds so much value to my life. This includes Melinda Demsky (and her beautiful family, Kate, Alex and Steve), Catherine Aquino (and her husband John and daughter, Valentina), Vanessa Taylor, Stephanie Goldsmith, Diane Drake, Chayse Dacoda, Shanna Rosen Bellot, Elaine Naspo, Patty Sachs, Kimberly Curtin, Rachel Bendavid, Kim Hudson, Diane Gross, Carole Kirschner, Kathie Fong Yoneda, Korinna Sehringer, Cayman Grant-City, and John Bassett.

I want to give a special thanks to Andy Elkin at CAA. You have been a light in my life since the day we met. Your support over the years has allowed me to shoot for the stars. I also want to thank Amie Yavor at CAA. I am so excited to be working with you.

I want to thank my clients. Each and every one of you has contributed to this process by sharing your talent, your emotions, and your stories with me.

I want to thank Karen Horne, my partner in crime for Writers on the Verge, for being one of the most talented and thoughtful executives that I've ever worked with. You are a gift. I want to thank Julie Ann Crommet for her savvy and being such an integral part of the Writers on the Verge program. I want to thank all of the present and former Writers on the Verge. Being a part of your growth and your journey is why I love what I do.

My extended circle of light includes all the authors whose books have contributed to the inspiration behind this concept. They include Steven Pressfield (*The War of Art, Turning Pro*), Brendon Burchard (*Millionaire Messenger*, *The Charge*), Phil Stutz and Barry Michels (*The Tools*), Shawn Achor (*The Happiness Advantage*), Dr. Wayne Dyer (*Wishes Fulfilled*), Deepak Chopra (*Spiritual Solutions and the 21-Day Meditation Challenge*), Arianna Huffington (*On Becoming Fearless*), Mary Goldenson (*It's Time, No One is Coming To Save You*), Seth

Godin (*Linchpin*), Daniel H. Pink (*Drive*) Jerry Weissman (*Presenting To Win*), LD Thompson (*The Message*), Marianne Williamson (*The Gift of Change*) and Tony Robbins (*Awaken The Giant Within*).

I want to thank the people and the places that provided the backdrop for the inspiration. They include Miraval, Esalen, Terranea, The Big Hawaiian Film Festival (Leo and Jan Sears) and The Wellness Inversion Retreat (Jade and Stephen Webber).

Lastly, I want to give a very special thank you to all of the people from Facebook, LinkedIn, and Twitter who filled out my questionnaire about life turning points. Your stories, even if they are not mentioned, provided so much value to the writing of this book. I give sincere gratitude for your courage in sharing your stories.

About the Author

International speaker Jen Grisanti is an acclaimed Story/Career Consultant at Jen Grisanti Consultancy, Inc. She is also a Writing Instructor for Writers on the Verge at NBC, a former studio executive, a blogger for The Huffington Post, and author of *Story Line: Finding Gold In Your Life Story* and *TV Writing Tool Kit: How To Write a Script That Sells.*

Twenty years ago, Grisanti started her career as an assistant to Aaron Spelling, who served as her mentor for 12 years. She quickly climbed the ranks and eventually ran Current Programs at Spelling Television Inc., covering all of Spelling's shows including *Beverly Hills 90210*, *Melrose Place*, and *Charmed*. In 2004, Grisanti was promoted to Vice President of Current Programs at CBS/Paramount, where she covered numerous shows including *Medium*, *Numbers*, *NCIS*, *4400*, and *Girlfriends*.

In January 2008, Grisanti launched Jen Grisanti Consultancy, Inc., a highly successful consulting firm dedicated to helping talented writers break into the industry. Drawing on her years of experience as a studio executive, where she gave daily notes to executive producers and showrunners, Grisanti personally guides writers to shape their material, hone their pitches, and focus their careers. Since launching her consulting firm, Grisanti has worked with more than 500 writers specializing in television, features, and novels. Due to her expertise and mentorship, thirty-four of her clients have staffed as writers on television shows, fourteen have sold pilots, and two of those pilots have gone to series.

Grisanti's brand focus is "Telling and Selling Your Story and Developing From Within."

As a way to inspire business owners and entrepreneurs, she currently offers the following presentations: "How To Give A Winning Pitch: Finding Your Voice, Story-Driven Success" and "Moving Beyond Your 'All Is Lost' Moment."

Grisanti also has a Storywise Podcast Series available on iTunes and via her website, www.jengrisanticonsultancy.com. The podcasts dig deep into our top storytellers' histories as a way to inform, motivate, and inspire listeners to go after their dreams.

Grisanti has taught classes for the TV Writers Summit, The Big Island Film Festival, Chicago Screenwriters Network, Scriptwriters Network, Screenwriting Network, Screenwriting Exp, The Great American Pitchfest, the Northwestern Screenwriter's Guild in Seattle, and the Alameda's Writer's Group. In addition, she has served on panels for the WGA, iTVFest, UFVA, PGA, and The Writer's Bootcamp, telling her story to inspire others.

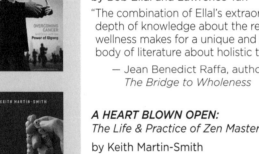

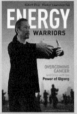

YEAR ZERO: *Time of the Great Shift*

by Kiara Windrider

"I can barely contain myself as I implode with gratitude for the gift of *Year Zero*! Every word resonates on a cellular level, awakening ancient memories and realigning my consciousness with an unshakable knowing that the best has yet to come. This is more than a book; it is a manual for building the new world!"

— Mikki Willis, founder, ELEVATE

ILAHINOOR: *Awakening the Divine Human*

by Kiara Windrider

"Ilahinoor is a truly precious and powerful gift for those yearning to receive and integrate Kiara Windrider's guidance on their journey for spiritual awakening and wisdom surrounding the planet's shifting process."

— Alexandra Delis-Abrams, Ph.D., author *Attitudes, Beliefs, and Choices*

THE MESSAGE: *A Guide to Being Human*

by LD Thompson

"Simple, profound, and moving! The author has been given a gift... a beautiful way to distill the essence of life into an easy-to-read set of truths, with wonderful examples along the way. Listen... for that is how it all starts."

— Lee Carroll, author, the *Kryon* series; co-author, *The Indigo Children*

SOPHIA—THE FEMININE FACE OF GOD:
Nine Heart Paths to Healing and Abundance

by Karen Speerstra

"Karen Speerstra shows us most compellingly that when we open our hearts, we discover the wisdom of the Feminine all around us. A totally refreshing exploration, and beautifully researched read."

— Michael Cecil, author, *Living at the Heart of Creation*

A FULLER VIEW: *Buckminster Fuller's Vision of Hope and Abundance for All*

by L. Steven Sieden

"This book elucidates Buckminster Fuller's thinking, honors his spirit, and creates an enthusiasm for continuing his work."

— Marianne Williamson, author, *Return To Love* and *Healing the Soul of America*

GAIA CALLS: *South Sea Voices, Dolphins, Sharks & Rainforests*

by Wade Daok

"Wade has the soul of a dolphin, and has spent a life on and under the oceans on a quest for deep knowledge. This is an important book that will change our views of the ocean and our human purpose."

— Ric O'Barry, author, *Behind the Dolphin Smile* and star of *The Cove,* which won the 2010 Academy Award for Best Documentary

1.800.833.5738 • 25% discount available online • www.divineartsmedia.com

Divine Arts sprang to life fully formed as an intention to bring spiritual practice into daily life.

Human beings are far more than the one-dimensional creatures perceived by most of humanity and held static in consensus reality. There is a deep and vast body of knowledge — both ancient and emerging — that informs and gives us the understanding, through direct experience, that we are magnificent creatures occupying many dimensions with untold powers and connectedness to all that is.

Divine Arts books and films explore these realms, powers, and teachings through inspiring, informative, and empowering works by pioneers, artists, and great teachers from all the wisdom traditions. We invite your participation and look forward to learning how we may serve you.

Onward and upward,
Michael Wiese, Publisher